LINEKER
GOLDEN BOOT

LINEKER
GOLDEN BOOT

Photographs by Bob Thomas

Text by Rob Hughes

Willow Books
Collins
8 Grafton Street, London W1
1987

Acknowledgements

We would like to thank John Dawes of the *Daily Star* and
Neville Chadwick for their help and co-operation in supplying
pictures for use in the book. Our thanks also to Everton FC and
David Smith of Leicester FC for helping to compile the statistics.

Willow Books
William Collins Sons & Co Ltd
London · Glasgow · Sydney
Auckland · Toronto · Johannesburg

First published in Great Britain 1987
© Oceania Investments BV/Bob Thomas 1987

British Library Cataloguing in Publication Data

Hughes, Rob
Lineker: golden boot.
1. Lineker, Gary 2. Soccer players —
Great Britain — Biography
I. Title II. Thomas, Bob
796.334'092'4   GV942.7.L5/

ISBN 0-00-218294-7

Designed by Sackville Design Group Ltd, 78 Margaret Street,
London W1N 7HB
Typeset in Plantin by Bookworm Typesetting, Manchester, and
Sackville Design Group Ltd

Printed and bound in Italy by New Interlitho SpA Milan

CONTENTS

1

THE
GIFT

*The colours are now Spanish, the style remains
English to the core.*

Cricket is another inbred Lineker trait. The brothers played initially for Caldecote Road Junior School (Gary front row, centre; Wayne standing behind his left ear). Below The footballer-cricketer shows the style of an opening bat who played for Midlands Schools U-15: "I was sure I was a better cricketer than footballer," recalls Gary. "I got bored fielding so I began keeping wicket. I'm a purist, I love to watch five-day Test matches."

At mother Margaret's knee: The first Gary Lineker left-foot volley at eighteen months. Eyes on the ball, high follow-through, a born stylist!

TIMING is Gary Lineker's business. Every working day, in training or matchplay, he practises being in the right place at the right time. He labours at what comes naturally.

We have all seen how uncannily he anticipates, how swiftly he moves, how decisively he finishes. Defenders are there to stop him at any cost but Lineker is like the Scarlet Pimpernel; he is here and then gone, leaving only the sting behind. So often his goals look simple, so often he repeats them in any company, on any stage. The trick, he says revealing nothing, is getting there.

Star quality is the wonder of modern soccer. Why, in a game designed for team effort, should the same individual rise above all efforts to destroy him when it matters most? If adrenaline heightens his senses, why not theirs? If he summons up greater concentration, finer sharpness when pressures mount, why don't they?

You may trace Gary Winston Lineker back to the cradle and beyond. Football runs in the family. Dad played reasonably well, Grandad played better and with that combination of speed and balance which is Lineker's forte today. Open the family album and there, at eighteen months, is Gary at his mother Margaret's knee, already with enthusiasm and timing for the ball. (Left foot, he notes!)

Love of sports, hereditary running speed (Gary was Leicestershire schools 400 metres champion), and a ball-player's eye gave him a choice of apprenticeships between football and cricket. He could now be Leicestershire, possibly even England, opening bat. He could, suggest some who have watched him compile century breaks at snooker, have become a pro on the green baize.

Yet soccer consumes him and the more he attacks it the more his timing seems brushed by destiny. Even Lineker could not have schemed to score the instant Leicester City's chief scout set eyes on him at the age of fourteen. He could not have plotted the opening he turned into a goal two minutes into his debut as a £2.2 million Barcelona player.

Above those, 11 June 1986 made one wonder if he has a pact with the great timekeeper in the sky. Lineker was in Monterrey, responding to England's desperate thirst for World Cup goals. While he was scoring a first-half hat-trick against Poland in Mexico, his business adviser Jon Holmes and accountant Peter Sutton were travelling from England to Barcelona to find out how much the Spanish club were prepared to pay him. "So Gary has three goals more," Barcelona's vice president Joan

The trappings of status. Lineker's strikes for club and country projected him towards two Adidas Golden Boots as top English League scorer and top World Cup scorer in 1986. His own boots, Quaser, were launched in 1987 in keeping with the style Gary and his wife Michelle are becoming accustomed to at home in Barcelona.

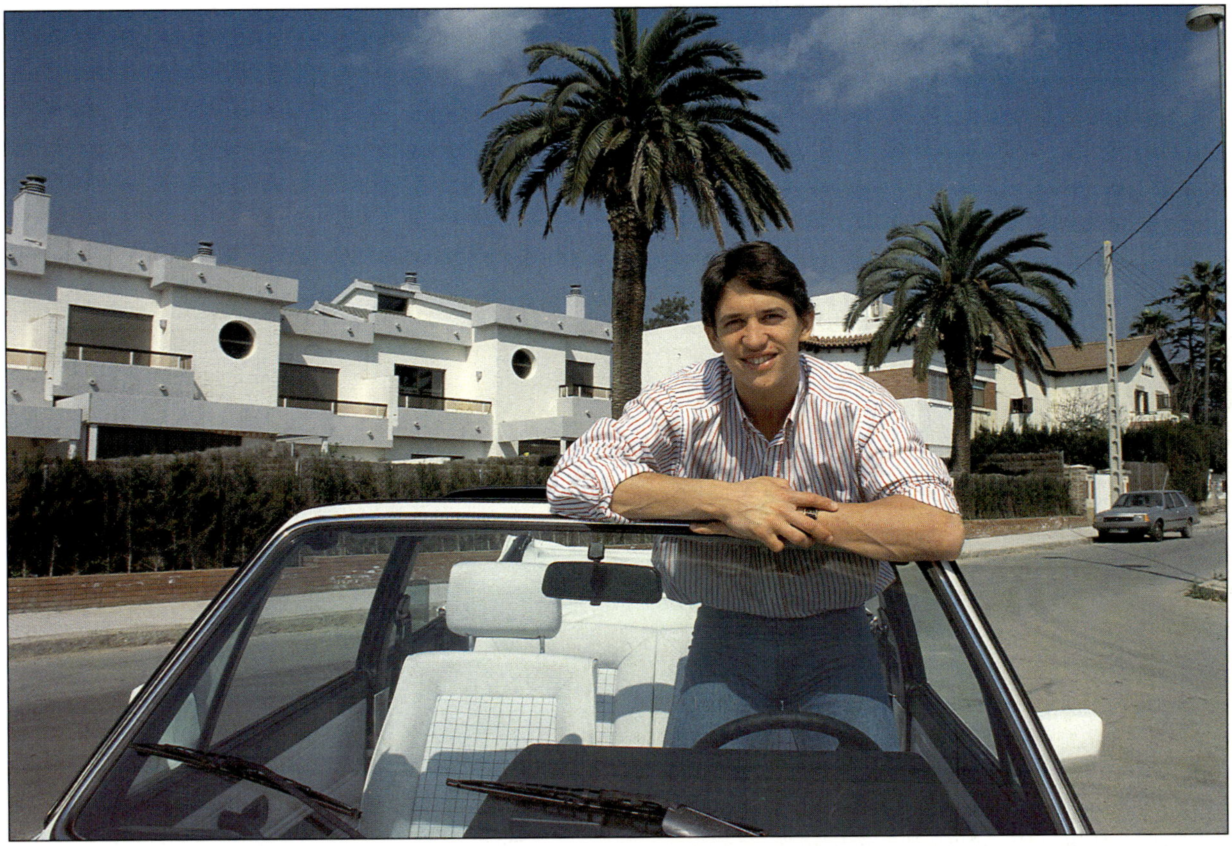

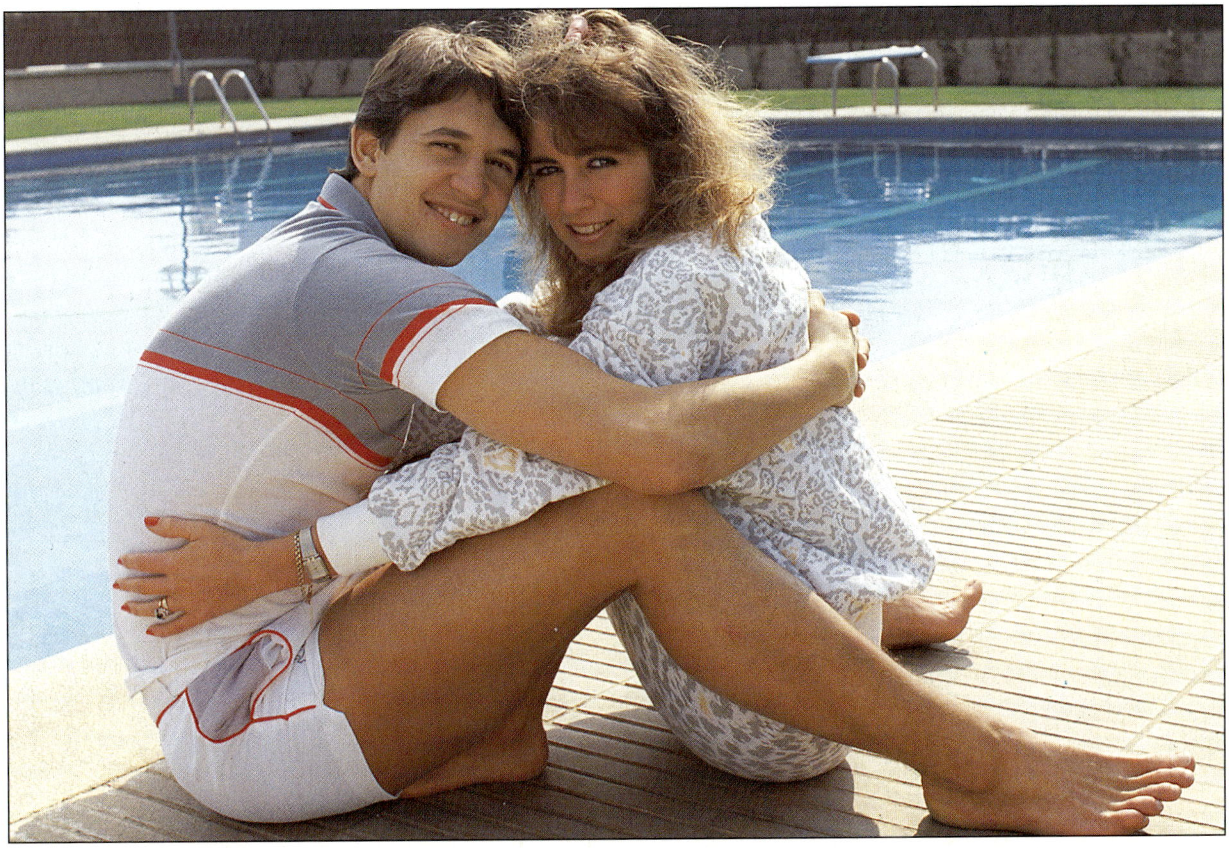

Gaspart greeted them. "Now you are going to ask more money?"

Mercenary, these Latins. The fact is, that particular incentive never occurred to Lineker. It could not have; he was unaware of Barcelona's offer until *after* the Poland match. Indeed, the full, untold sequence of negotiations reveals a great deal about Gary Lineker's attitude, about his trust in family and business partners, and about the sheer coincidence which Barcelona took to be another example of his inspired timing.

The Catalans made a tentative approach for Lineker two months earlier when Gaspart spoke to Everton manager Howard Kendall. Everton would sell if the price was right, but Kendall agonized over fear of unsettling Lineker during the championship run-in and before the FA Cup

Opposite Oh to be in England now that winter's here:
Lineker in pensive mood during a Leicester v Forest
match in April 1985, dreaming perhaps of warmer climates.

The games people play. Gary's judgement and timing
extend to the snooker table where he has regularly
practised with his friend Willie Thorne. On this
occasion, Thorne had invited Lineker to a Go-Kart
race. Gary declined and was thus available on cue for his
next professional duty.

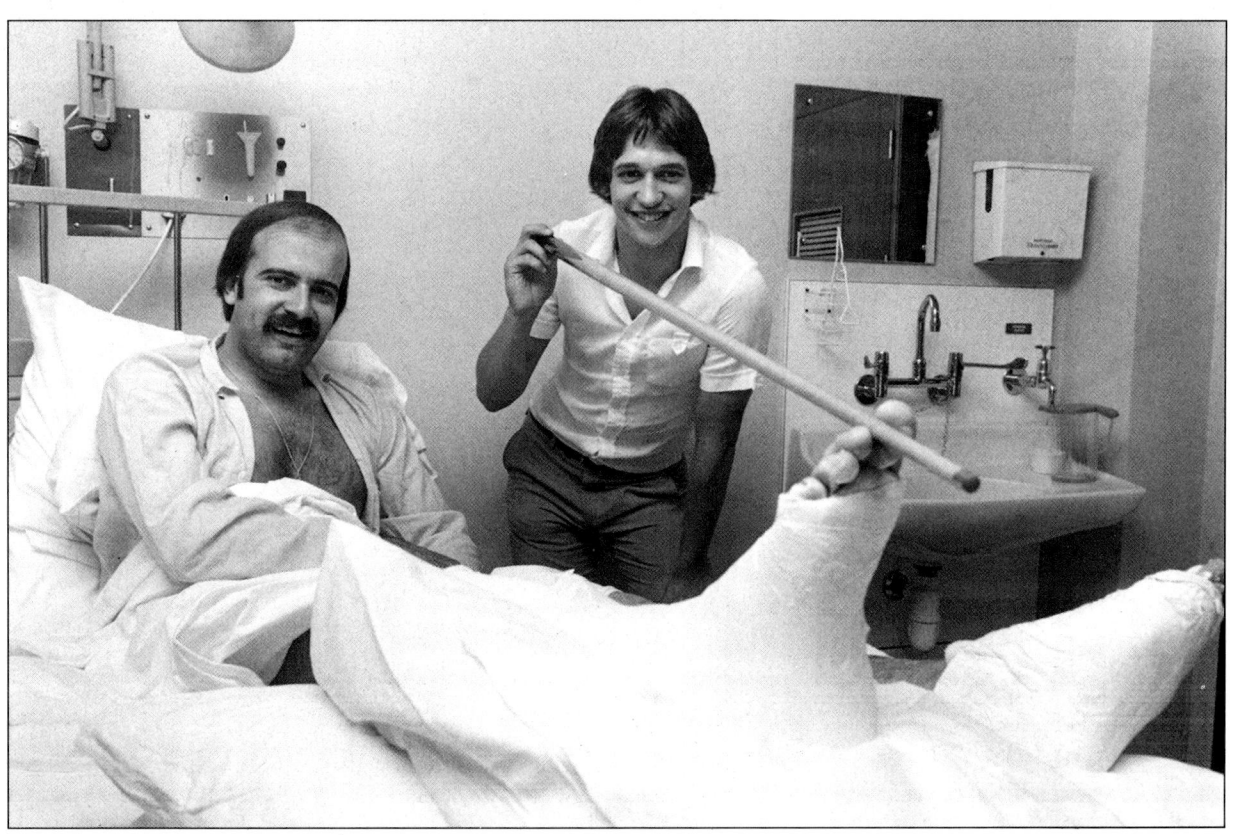

Goals attract cameras like moths to a flame. Above *After Lineker's Wembley hat-trick for England against Turkey in 1985.* Right *All good publicity leads to Barcelona.*

The Hand of God shakes the hand of the Golden Boot: Maradona congratulates Lineker, whose six goals topped the 1986 World Cup scoring. Left Gary in solitude in the chapel inside Barcelona's Nou Camp stadium.

*Home is where your swimming pool is – and inevitably
for Gary and Michelle Lineker home in Barcelona is
open-house to a television crew. Promotion is part and
parcel of the job.*

final. Ultimately, he felt honour-bound to inform the player. Lineker concentrated on the job in hand, scoring five times in two remaining League games and once at Wembley. Alas, Everton finished second to Liverpool in both.

The Barcelona trail had gone cold, presumed dead. Gaspart failed to come through with two promised phone calls and Lineker took off for Mexico believing Barcelona might have switched to Ian Rush.

However, on 6 June Holmes was called from the golf course to hear from Kendall that Barcelona were back and in earnest. It was the Friday of England's depressing goalless draw with Morocco. Holmes, after consulting Gary's fiancée Michelle and his father Barry, elected to keep the news quiet until after the Poland match.

That was exactly as Lineker wanted. He was euphoric after the three goals against Poland when Michelle told him of Barcelona's offer but his response was: "Leave it to Jon, I'll talk when we've finished here." It would have pleased Bobby Robson, the England manager, who was already having kittens over the turmoil surrounding Terry Butcher's move from Ipswich to Glasgow Rangers. It did not please Barcelona, who expected Holmes to sign on Lineker's behalf. Gary, after all, is a player – why would he want time to think about it? This is Barcelona calling, the club of players' dreams.

Holmes dutifully took the contract, unsigned, back to Leicester. A summit was held next morning on the lawn of Michelle's parents' home. Michelle, her father Roger Cockayne, and Gary's brother Wayne (standing in for their father who had to man the family fruit stall) agreed to cancel plans to fly the contract out to Mexico. Instead, they asked Barcelona to await the hero's return.

Even that had clandestine undertones. Lineker finished his World Cup with six of England's seven goals. The Golden Boot had outscored Maradona, Butragueno, Careca, Preben-Elkjaer, Altobelli . . . all of them. The Press was buzzing with transfer speculation.

Pan Am helped to spirit Lineker through London airport to a hotel where he stayed two hours before doubling back to catch the shuttle home to Liverpool. He remained there for two days, finalizing small print by phone. Finally, one more summit wrapped things up over lunch at London's Connaught Hotel. The buyers, José Nuñez, son of Josep Lluis Nuñez, Joan Gaspart and Terry Venables (president, vice president and coach of Barcelona FC) put up £2.2 million for the transfer and £1.5 million gross over six years for Lineker. The sellers, Philip Carter, Jim Greenwood and Howard Kendall (chairman, secretary and manager of Everton FC) accepted. And Lineker and his business manager wondered, slightly sheepishly, whether they had stung Barcelona for rather too expensive a wine after Gaspart had extravagantly invited them to name the celebration vintage.

After all, this market trader's son who had taken his first kick at eighteen months on a Leicester park must not twenty five years later break the bank of new paymasters who were offering to make him a millionaire.

2

HOME BASE

*Home town hero: Gary Lineker in Leicester City
blue beginning the career where he was born and
bred and his talent nurtured.*

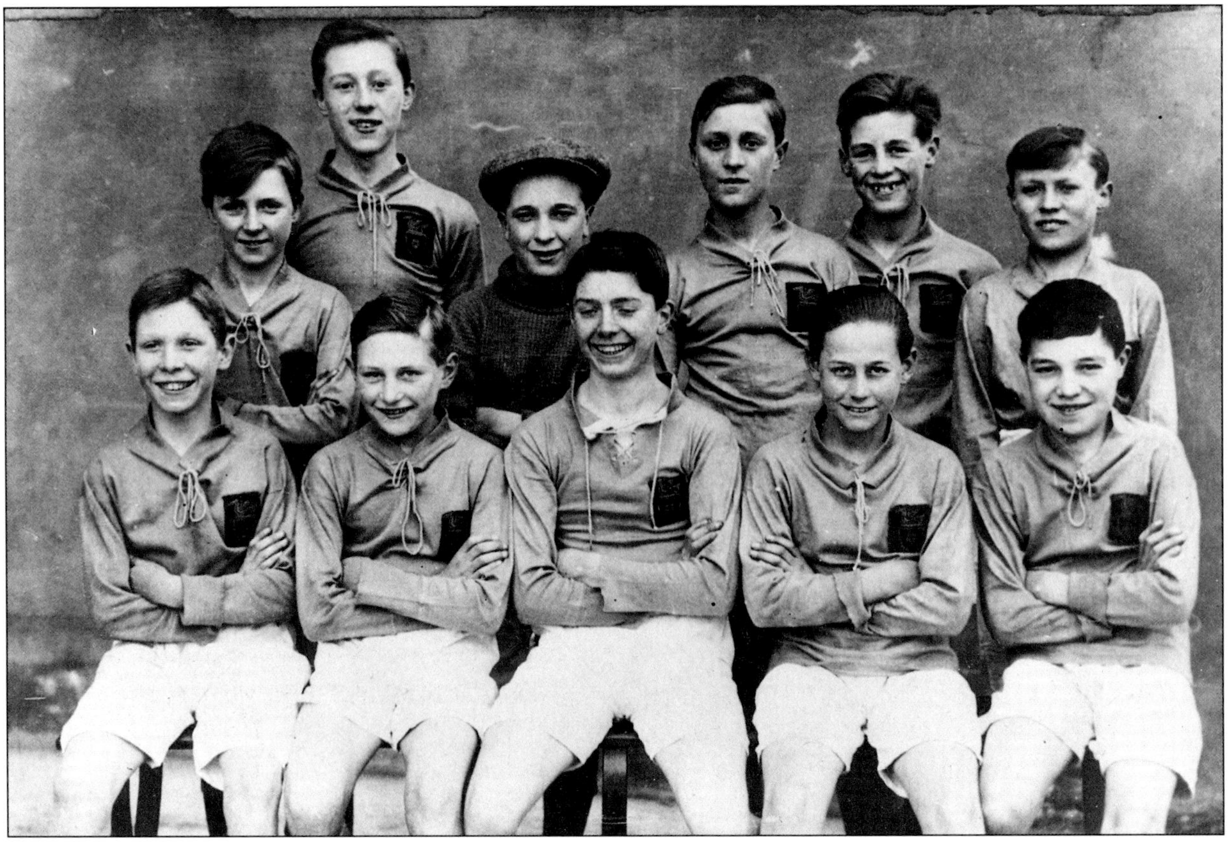

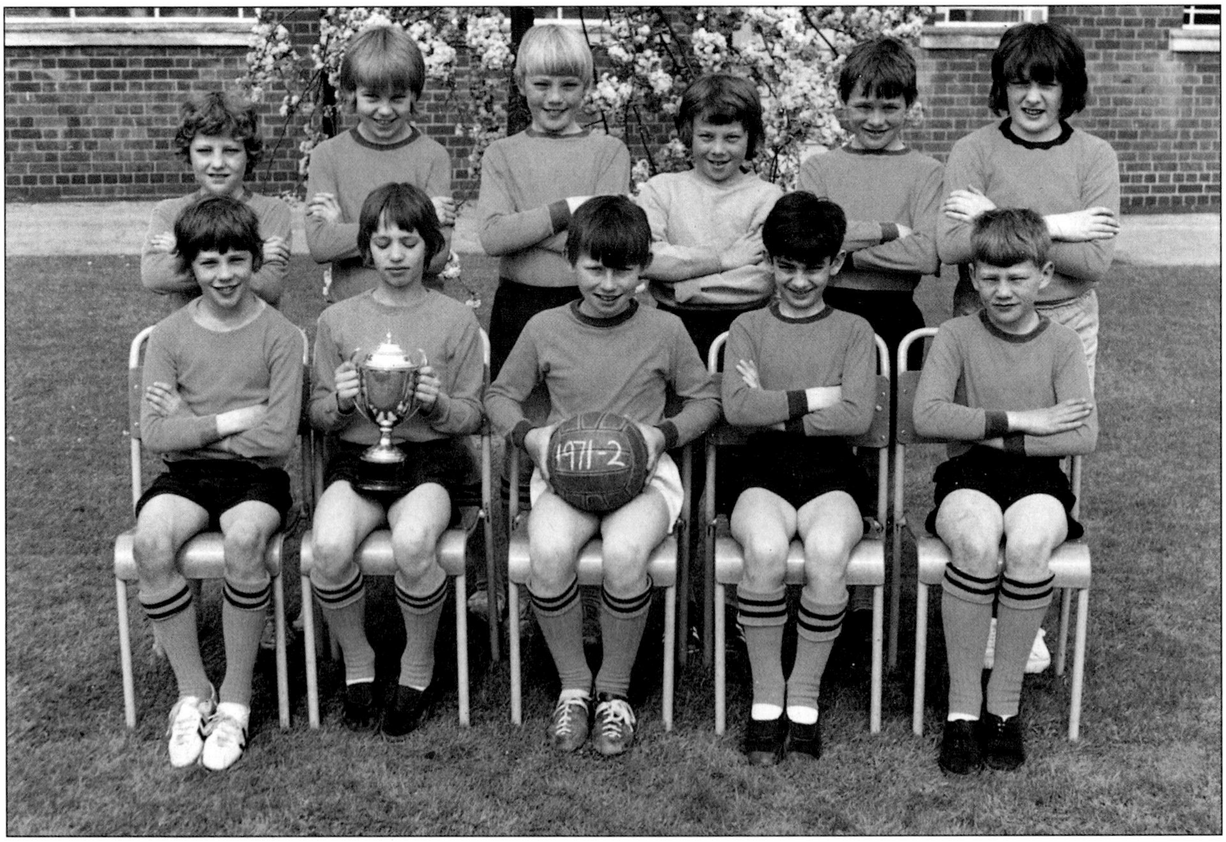
1971-2

"Lineker (St George's). One of the finest outside-rights that Leicester has produced. He is a splendid winger, with wonderful ball control." *7 March 1925*

THE first tributes to Lineker talent are to be found in yellowing newspaper archives in the city where the Linekers have been footballers for almost as many generations as they have traded in the local market. Harold Lineker, the nimble Leicester Schoolboys winger of the 1920s, is Gary's grandfather. And, although the old legs are unsteady at times, although Parkinson's disease affects the speech, Grandad Lineker is still a root source of Gary's motivation, still a knowlegeable well of sensible opinion to whom the young superstar turns.

"Grandad lives for me," observes Gary without attempting to hide the sentimental chord between the two. Over the phone between Barcelona and Leicester things are a little difficult, with emotion getting the better of the old man. But back home during flying visits to play for England, Gary and his grandfather pick up where they left off.

"How're they treating you in Barcelona, Gary?" asks the head of the family. "Giving you a bit of stick are they?"

"A bit of stick, Grandad, yes."

Man to man they agree that you cannot expect to play up front for the richest team in the world and not get a bit of stick. A price without complaint, though afterwards, while the two men are engrossed in debate about hard times, Gary's elegant, strong grandmother Alice speaks quietly about her fears of some Spanish boot cutting short Gary's career. "He always says not to worry Nanna, they're pussy cats out there. But you know what makes us proud? Gary's not come back one little bit bigheaded. And with all that kicking he hasn't once retaliated. He's still never been booked."

Gary has always said that his parents, Barry and Margaret, were the major influences on his career. And that is right, both in the way he means it to acknowledge their guidance and support, and in agreement with an observation by the late Bill Shankly that "mothers and fathers, not coaches, make great players".

The footballing schooldays of Linekers down the ages. Top *Front row extreme left, Harold Lineker, flying winger of Leicester Schoolboys in 1925.* Bottom *Gary with the trophy and brother Wayne to his right in the 1972 Caldecote Road Junior School team which won the local Billing Cup.*

Gary Lineker, eyes on the ball, an early study in Leicester City of the concentration that locks out all distractions.

*Chelsea, in yellow, hunt Lineker in threes
during a Second Division game at
Leicester in 1983.*

*Meeting soccer's hard men on the way up.
Lineker about to be challenged by Graham Roberts of Spurs
during Leicester's 2-0 FA Cup semi-final defeat in 1982.*

Who shall buy? Gary Lineker, future Golden Boot, selling Golden Delicious on the family market stall in Leicester. Brother Wayne covers up.

A winning pair: On Gary's twenty first birthday, his father Barry brought home his prize catch in a major angling contest.

Shankly was fascinated by family trees, and by sons whose exceptional skills are sometimes throwbacks to previous generations. Gary's father passed on the addiction to soccer to both his sons. He himself played with all the enthusiasm in the world, but was not so blessed with the winning combination of explosive speed, natural balance, and thoroughbred timing. Besides, Dad went to grammar school after passing the 11-plus, and Leicestershire grammar schools frowned on soccer.

Wayne, Gary's younger brother by seventeen months, was a quick, artful winger but in contrast to Gary was volatile. He would erupt if any full-back upset him. Wayne, now twenty five and father to the first of the next generation of Lineker sons (an equable child by all accounts), is outwardly content at the way his and his brother's lives are panning out. He works the market alongside his father.

Well, you would not expect lightning to strike twice in the same place, or would you? There is every sign that it has in the Lineker family – in a straight line from grandfather to grandson. Michelle, who married Gary in 1986, is struck by the similarities between Gary and his grandad. "He's a carbon copy of his grandad in terms of personality," she believes.

"And I think we're just beginning to appreciate how good Grandad might have been if he'd had the same opportunities as a player."

Michelle is intrigued by the 1925 newspaper clipping describing Harold Lineker as a star of the Leicester Schoolboys who triumphed through five rounds of the English Schools FA Shield before losing on a replay to the all-powerful West Ham. The reports are littered with references to the slippery but diminutive H. Lineker. Push Harold hard, and he admits:

"I never thought until recently that I must have been fairly decent. It's only through Gary that I've started thinking this. Nobody ever caught me if the ball was played in front of me, but it never struck me as anything special. St George's was a small school – 150 pupils, half of them girls. We carried our own goalposts to Welford Road to play."

Harold remembers now his father telling him, years after the event, that one of the regional schools selectors had revealed that he was the fastest player they had had. And only in retrospect does it strike him that regular selection, from a school whose team made bottom spot in the fifth and final division of Leicester Schools League its own, was something of an achievement.

However, being so small and slight, Harold's father took him out of school at fourteen to give him "a couple of years in the fresh air on the market". The day after he left he rose at seven to cut flowers. The one momento of Harold Lineker's schooldays is a sepia-toned photo of the class of 1925 – he is on the right, front row of the Leicester Schools side that went all the way to London in the Schools Shield.

"Grandad was obviously built similar to me," notes Gary. "We're late developers. I was just under 5ft 6in and less than nine stones when I left school at sixteen. I used to get knocked off the ball all the time, I never professed to be the most skilled player in the world, so it wasn't surprising I was hardly flooded with offers."

Indeed, Leicester City's was the only apprenticeship that came his way. And they had a gentle nudge from Harold Lineker, a man self-effacing about his own talent but no slouch in singing the praises of no. 1 grandson. In Harold's eyes, Tom Finney was the finest two-footed footballer on earth, at least until George Best. Being able to use the left and the right is a diminishing art, but it is no coincidence that Gary snaps up chances without hesitation on either foot.

"We started them very early on this," recalls Grandad Lineker. "We'd go out for the day and straight away a ball would come out. And, whenever Gary or Wayne received it, either their dad or myself would tell

The effort, the pain, the concentration of Second Division days were worthwhile when, as in these photographs, they led to Leicester's 5-0 drubbing of Wolves.

them they didn't want to be kicking with their right foot if the ball came to the left."

The suggestion that Gary *lacks* instant first touch on the ball surprises Harold. "You can't play unless you can control the ball," he stresses. His opaque eyes come as close as they ever will to annoyance: "That's wrong about our Gary, and he sells himself short if he agrees with you! Look at Liverpool. They simply pass the ball accurately . . . as soon as you start to get clever at the game, you get beat.

"Gary may not elaborate a lot, but he can slide five, six yards to a ball. His anticipation is remarkable, really. Okay, he's my grandson, but you've challenged me now. The greatest tribute I can pay Gary – the reason he's such a good player – is how quickly he controls the ball from any angle. If it comes chest high it's down to his feet straight away. It's fantastic, he must visualize things before he gets the ball, he sometimes runs fifteen yards into space and looks as if he's waiting; then it's straight in the net."

Being on the right spot at the opportune time is an old Lineker habit. Grandad was there the moment Leicester spotted Gary. It was not surprising; the total audience at Sunday games Gary played, morning and

First-footing for an apprentice:
Left *Lineker's debut for Leicester against Oldham Athletic at Filbert Street on 1 January 1979.* Right *Contesting a high ball with Sunderland's Tim Gilbert also in 1979, showing how slender Lineker was. He began his League career at 5ft 7in and 9½ stones and is now 5ft 10in and 12½ stones.*

afternoon for different parks' teams, was seldom bigger than a posse. And Harold was always there.

He claims he did not actually know Ray Shaw, Leicester City's late chief scout, whom he happened to be standing beside during an Under-14 match between Aylestone Park and Wadkins. "I'd seen this chap at quite a few matches," Harold recalls, "and this particular afternoon he said to me: 'That's the one I've got my eye on, the little Aylestone lad up front.'

"Gary scored that very moment, and the chap turned to me saying: 'I told you!' "

Ray Shaw introduced himself then as Leicester chief scout, Harold let it be known that the boy in question was his grandson, and Shaw replied: "I'm very impressed, the way he got that ball under control." Harold contained his excitement until he got home, but he began to bump into Shaw at more and more Aylestone matches. Doubtless the scout heard more than enough about the 161 goals (yes, 161) Gary once scored in one season for his school Under-11 team. Doubtless, too, the scout did his own homework but you can just imagine the grandfather, in his innocence of course, passing remarks like: "People are always saying he

Right foot this time?
Gary poses to shoot against
Spurs in 1984.

Tottenham's Paul Miller is given a foretaste of the
elusive Lineker movement as he suddenly changes
balance and direction.

"Always on the floor!" the Leicester critics
jibed. "See how quickly he bounces up again,"
said his fans.

The shot is delivered, the ball is fractionally wide or saved, and that secondary emotion of the goal-scorer – frustration – is written all over him.

My hero. Gary spent his schooldays and his apprentice years in awe of the flair of Frank Worthington, one of the most naturally gifted forwards of his generation.

The first and the 100th goal in Leicester colours. Inset *Sheer euphoria lifts Gary after his goal against Sunderland in October 1979. The response is cooler by April 1985 when a goal against Nottingham Forest clocks up his 25th that season.*

spends too much time on the floor, but look how quick he gets up", "He's small now, but his father was the same, I was the same, we shot up in our late teens", "See that speed? Gary's the schools sprint champion. He's fantastic at cricket, too. Mike Turner's trying to get him to sign for the County you know".

The promise was there. The talent was there. "As a boy, Gary came regularly to our indoor coaching," recalls Mike Turner, the Leicestershire County Cricket Club secretary-manager. "I always felt soccer would take precedence, but had he chosen cricket I suspect Gary would have matured into almost as successful an all-rounder as he's proved at football. He has balance and movement which are part of the natural player's aptitude, and always came full of enthusiasm."

In bygone days, when the sports respected their seasons, Lineker

Newcastle taking the strain in 1984. Glenn Roeder is beaten in the air, and Wesley Saunders is outpaced and outmuscled on the ground.

Almost unnoticed, players have become walking advertisements. Stand still and the brewery company gets its money's worth; move on and the action blurs the message.

Left *Early international experience as Lineker is challenged by Australian goalkeeper Greg Woodhouse during a Leicester City v Australia friendly in 1980.* Right *More familiar territory, against Leeds United.*

The Leicester "wall" of 1981, left to right: Ian Wilson, Andy Peake (considered at that time to be the outstanding prospect), Gary Lineker, Billy Gibson, Keith Robson and Jim Melrose.

might never have had to choose. He might have followed in the footsteps of the Compton brothers, of Patsy Hendren, Joe Hulme, Willie Watson and company who bestrode the heights of both sports – cricket in the summer and football in winter. The seasons blurred, the breed vanished, and although Leicestershire revived it in the 1970s with both Graham Cross and Chris Balderstone returning to County cricket in their thirties after full-time soccer careers Turner doubts it could ever happen again.

Turner has recommended Lineker to the MCC so that he might indulge in his lost sport as an occasional club cricketer. The occasions will be collectors' items, rarities to put it mildly. And even if soccer leaves him unbroken, the chances of an Indian summer's cricket are remote.

All this is no reflection on his physique. As Grandad foretold, Gary enjoyed his growth spurt in his late teens. Aided and abetted by high-protein foods, and two to three hours a day weightlifting, he gained over three inches in height and over two stones in weight by the time he made his debut for Leicester City, as an eighteen-year-old, on 1 January 1979.

City was then a struggling Second Division side, one ready to pitch a couple of likely lads into the survival effort. Very soon the whole of Leicester were shouting the name of their wonder boy from the rooftops. It was *Andy Peake!*

A year younger than Lineker, but bloodied in the first team that same month, Peake was an England youth international and a midfield prospect of spectacularly precocious vision. "There are footballers, good footballers, and then there are the Andy Peakes," drooled Leicester's normally ferocious Scottish manager Jock Wallace. Jock's style was a cavalry charge, his demands were obedience, exhaustion and players who understood that "there's only one good fertilizer – blood and sweat".

Yet it was not so much Lineker, with his eagerness to please and his obvious raw courage, that Wallace built Leicester's future on. "The boy Peake has that certain something that jumps off the pitch and hits you in the eye," said Wallace. "I promise you this lad is going all the way, and that means lots of caps."

Lineker readily concedes that he was "nothing outstanding", that he "just improved gradually", and that Peake was everything Wallace and all the senior players eulogized. Mark Wallington, for example, the City goalkeeper who experienced thirty nine players in front of him during his first hundred games at Leicester, wrote in the club's programme in April 1982: "Out of all the bright, talented youngsters we have, Andy Peake is my particular tip for the top. He is aggressive, he has vision, he has tremendous stamina."

Before the parting of the ways, Andy Peake (left) and Gary Lineker (below). They had grown up in the Leicester youth team together, and Peake had been the more visionary talent everyone anticipated would become a great international, but look at them now.

Opposite *Men of Leicester at both ends of England celebrations. Peter Shilton and Gary Lineker after the 5-0 World Cup slaughter of Turkey in which Shilton became the most capped English goalkeeper and Lineker scored three goals.* Below *Back home for a rare visit from Barcelona, Lineker among City supporters.*

umbro
umbro

LEICESTER
CITY F.C.
LEICESTER
CITY F.C.
LEICESTER CITY

*Goals are not the only memories from Leicester days.
Try forgetting the force with which a defender like Manchester
United's Graeme Hogg comes in from behind.*

Wallington, rarely for those days, also suspected there was a second VIP maturing at Filbert Street. "Gary Lineker has developed both mentally and physically," added the Leicester captain. "He has the heart of a lion and will run forever."

Hindsight suggests that he who waits wins. It is football's familiar pattern, the schoolboy and youth high flier being overtaken to full honours by the young man who persevered. That pattern is often unfathomable, bedevilled by the vagaries of youth, by the luck of injuries, by shifting team demands and the interminable managerial merry-go-round.

Jock Wallace, the volatile sergeant major, was replaced by the soothing Gordon Milne in August 1982. Perhaps Peake was stimulated by being driven over sand dunes. Perhaps Lineker needed time. Perhaps Wallace misused Lineker's phenomenal pace, which at eighteen was measured at 10.5 seconds for 100 metres (though Lineker himself says that being used as a winger for the first thirty League games did him no harm).

What is fact is that Lineker and Peake were sold by Leicester within weeks of one another in the summer of 1985. Lineker fetched £800,000 (and later an additional £250,000) from Everton, the League champions, and Peake moved on to Second Division Grimsby Town for £100,000, though he later rejoined the First Division with Charlton Athletic.

Lineker became top scorer at a World Cup, Peake still awaits the fulfilment of one England cap. We will find some of the positive reasons for Lineker's continuing rise in later chapters, but it is significant that Leicester, a relatively unpretentious club from a city not noted either for seething ambition or for the kind of harsh inner city deprivation that sometimes breeds "winners", has produced the two key players at either end of its national team. Lineker is our marksman, Peter Shilton commands the opposite role.

Lineker believes one vital clue to that lies in the coaching structure at Leicester. "The best coach for me was the first one I had at Leicester," he reflects. "George Dewis used to take us apprentices for two and a half hours every day, and all he did was *finishing*. Strikers against goalkeepers. George was the one who always said you can do it. He had more belief than I did, he was always showing me things like runs to the near post. Shilts and I often talk about this when we room together for England, and we agree that George, showing us what he knew best, really sharpened our game."

George Dewis? A familiar name to Lineker's grandfather. By coincidence (or was it timing?) Dewis and Lineker were war-time partners in the Royal Army Service Corps. Dewis, like many a Football League soccer professional, served as a PT instructor (a must for the Army soccer squad) while Lineker served as a weapons training instructor.

They came together when the Company Btn, short of a right-half, put Lineker down as reserve. "I'll be no use to you," warned the thirty one-year-old Lineker, "I've not kicked a ball for ten years. I've no place among all those professionals." Happy Harry, as he was nicknamed, was nevertheless co-opted, pressed into service in a position he had never played before and among a team including several internationals. He stayed in the team for two years, eventually using his pace up the right wing to serve a Manchester City centre-forward called George Dewis.

"I shouldn't say so," Harold muses, "but do you know those chaps could pass a ball so well it seemed a piece of cake. On a good day I rarely got caught." Thirty years later, youth coach Dewis found himself putting the same belief into an offspring of Happy Harry Lineker, a boy who could cut his teeth on goals.

3

£1,000,000 GEM

The new beginning, as an Evertonian,
in August 1985.

Manager Howard Kendall (left) and secretary Jim Greenwood making sure that Everton get their man. The signing of contracts in June 1985.

Opposite *A first hand on Everton silverware, Lineker with Trevor Steven and the Charity Shield won by beating Manchester United 2-0 at Wembley.* Below *The fury of a home debut, also won 2-0, for Everton against West Bromwich Albion.*

ITis said that an oyster takes seven years to produce a medium-sized pearl. Leicester City took seven seasons to polish Gary Lineker into a medium-sized goalscoring gem.

They put steaks into his body, slow-maturing confidence into his mind, and clung for as long as possible to his goals which for Leicester meant the difference between First and Second Division status. By the summer of 1985, the lure of the marketplace became irresistible.

Lineker had reached the milestone of 100 goals in 215 appearances when Everton bought him. As with all precious objects, the price raised some eyebrows including, in this case, the occupants of no. 10 Downing Street. The Prime Minister herself took an interest in the £800,000 (plus a percentage of any resale figure which eventually pushed the fee beyond the million-pound mark) Everton paid to Leicester.

The transfer came after the most horrifying spring in English sporting history. The Bradford fire, the death of a Birmingham fan caused by rioting Leeds hooligans, the slaughter of thirty nine spectators at the Heysel Stadium in Belgium, all happened in May. Lineker's transfer was settled on 23 July, and on 30 July Mrs Thatcher emphasized her government's demands for identity cards to be carried by football supporters.

The leading soccer administrators present, including Everton chair-

Two's company. Gary Gillespie introduces Lineker to the stifling attentions of close marking in the Liverpool-Everton derby. Not close enough: Everton win 2-0 at Anfield.

Opposite above *He went that way! Lineker outwits Manchester United's Graeme Hogg (falling) and Jesper Olsen.*

Opposite below *Now it's the turn of Martin Keown of Arsenal (later Aston Villa) to feel the Lineker pace.*

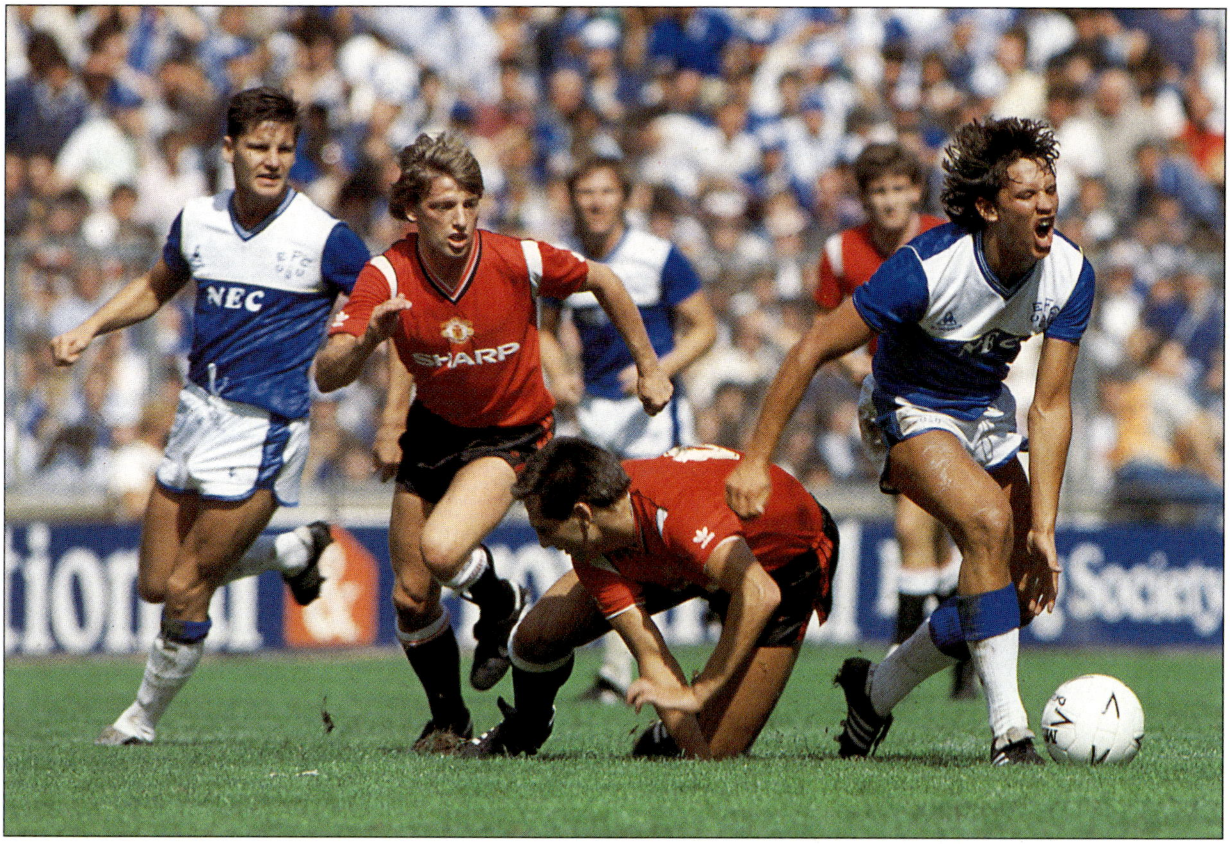
NEC
SHARP

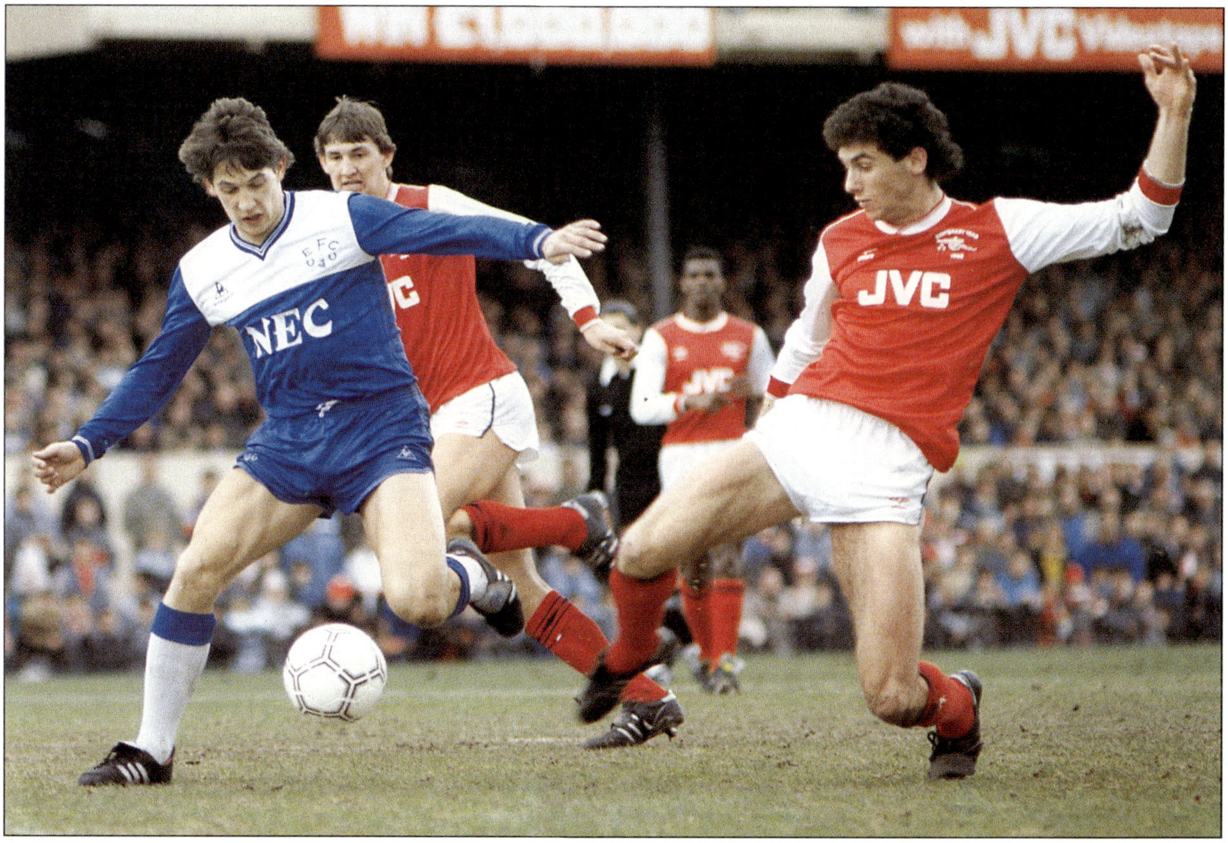
NEC
JVC

Everton exploited, more than Leicester ever had, Lineker's ability to head winning goals. It was not, manager Kendall says, a case of great leaps, but of his timing, bravery, instincts and acrobatics to capitalize on accurate crosses.

Manchester United suffered at awkward heights. Below Lineker scored against them in December 1985 with an astonishing flick-header. Right He connects with an overhead kick despite the raised boot of Norman Whiteside.

man Philip Carter who later became Football League president, pleaded poverty. They asked for a government subsidy towards the cost of combating hooliganism and improving ground safety. Mrs Thatcher gave them tea but little sympathy; she had seen the fee involved in the Lineker move and gave the impression that a sport which could afford £800,000 for one player could find the cash to put its house in order.

This is a common misconception among those who pay passing interest to football affairs. At any time, the vast majority of clubs live beyond their means. Indeed, the very day Lineker's transfer was decided a business survey calculated that only thirty six of the ninety two League clubs were out of the red for that financial year. The truth is, even First Division clubs like Leicester sell to survive, and Everton were in a unique position to pay a price that kept one of the country's leading goalscorers in Britain (albeit for just one year). Everton had just won both the League Championship and the European Cup Winners' Cup and had reached the FA Cup final: they had two options on the profits reaped in that rare season, either invest through the transfer market or surrender the bulk of the money in capital gains tax. They chose to buy Lineker.

"I felt Gary on the market was too good a chance to miss," explains Howard Kendall, the Everton manager. "He came here as our record signing, but the big question mark from my point of view was that Andy

Again Manchester United are the enemy, again Graeme Hogg is left marking time and space as Lineker speeds away with the ball. "He's always mobile," notes Kendall. "Very important that."

How does Lineker escape his markers? Martin Hodge, the Sheffield
Wednesday goalkeeper, is left exposed. Two goals against Wednesday were, Lineker feels,
the turning point in Everton fans accepting him as the replacement for Andy Gray.

Gray was really popular here. Andy had just had two tremendous seasons, the fans loved him, and I had to make a decision."

Kendall sold Gray to Aston Villa for £150,000. In cold logic, Lineker for Gray was sound business – buying in a younger, fitter, faster predator to replace an ageing Scots warhorse whose ankles had absorbed too many punishing skirmishes. Statistics are a crude, but inevitable measure applied to strikers and where Lineker had scored 72 goals in three League seasons Gray had accumulated 26, where Lineker was fit for 115 games Gray could manage only 86.

A man's value is tied to his athletic prime, and Lineker knows his marketability will one day decline as Gray's was doing when their paths crossed at Everton. It is part and parcel of the occupation and a manager who allows sentiment to sway his judgement will disappear quicker than the players.

Even so, parting with Gray was an emotional challenge for Kendall, a test of how dearly he wanted Lineker. When Kendall bought Gray from Wolves in November 1983 his managerial future, and the futures of some

For once Lineker is back-up, merely watching and waiting as Graeme Sharp (partially hidden by the post) scores amid mass confusion in the Manchester United goalmouth.

Liverpool's Mark Lawrenson, acknowledged as possibly the fastest defender in the League, takes the man as well as the ball as he crash-tackles Lineker during the 1986 FA Cup final. The tackle, the follow-through, and the painful grounding are captured in three colour frames. Below right A painful reminder of Lineker's previous meeting with Lawrenson, a fractured rib during their League match at Liverpool three months before the final. Even with that injury, Lineker completed the match.

Aerial supremacy. Through speed of thought, and by diving in where others might hesitate, Lineker bisects the Luton centre-backs Mal Donaghy and Steve Foster (headband) to head the winning goal of the 1986 FA Cup sixth-round replay over goalkeeper Les Sealey.

of his players, were jeopardized by the team's struggle near the First Division relegation zone. Kendall himself acknowledges that Gray, with his aggressive, positive attitude, stimulated a revival which led Everton to win the FA Cup that season and to storm the First Division and Europe the next. Possibly only Gray and Kendall know how often the centre-forward reached for painkillers to lay his vulnerable ankles on the line for Everton FC.

Going up to Gray's new home on Merseyside in the spring of 1985 to tell him the club had found a fresher goalscorer was, by any standards, a trial for Kendall. The other side was the euphoria in welcoming Gary Lineker to the fold.

Lineker and Everton looked natural partners. He finished his only season there with thirty eight goals from fifty two League and Cup appearances, a ratio only Francis Lee (Manchester City), Ron Davies (Southampton), Bob Latchford (Everton), Ian Rush (Liverpool) and Clive Allen (Tottenham) have approached in twenty years of First Division football.

Yet Lineker's goals were amassed while he and Everton probed for a rapport. The end product of his art may be a knack, an instinct, but that requires feeding. Everton, as Howard Kendall points out, had to change a winning formula.

"Players determine style," says Kendall. "Before Gary came we shared the goals more, and we've done that since he left. Our build-up was slower, we put more players into the penalty box. With Heath or Sharp we played it more to feet, whereas with Gary we became a bit more direct, using his pace to knock balls beyond the back four. When you've got a Sheedy on the ball, he sees the opportunities to use the direct ball for Gary to make runs into the channel between the centre-half and the full-back."

Kendall knew what his £800,000 was buying. "Gary's always been *alive* in the box," says the manager. "He's very rarely static. Very important, that. He's always moving into spaces, into good positions. He's alive all the time and really, really sharp off the blocks. He was renowned for this tremendous pace, but if anything surprised me a little bit it was that a large percentage of his goals here came from headers. He wasn't noted for that previously, but the headed goals came from his quickness and sharpness; it wasn't a case of tremendous leaps in the air, more a question of good crossers putting in the balls which he capitalized on whether in the air or on the ground."

Lineker surprised himself with so many headed goals, but he knows

In sequence, a Wembley goal from beginning to end. Left Alan Hansen is first to sense the danger as Lineker outpaces him. He moves at lightning speed towards the right of Bruce Grobbelaar's goal, draws a despairing dive from the goalie, and sidefoots the ball beneath him. Everton's congratulations were short-lived as Liverpool came from behind to win the Cup.

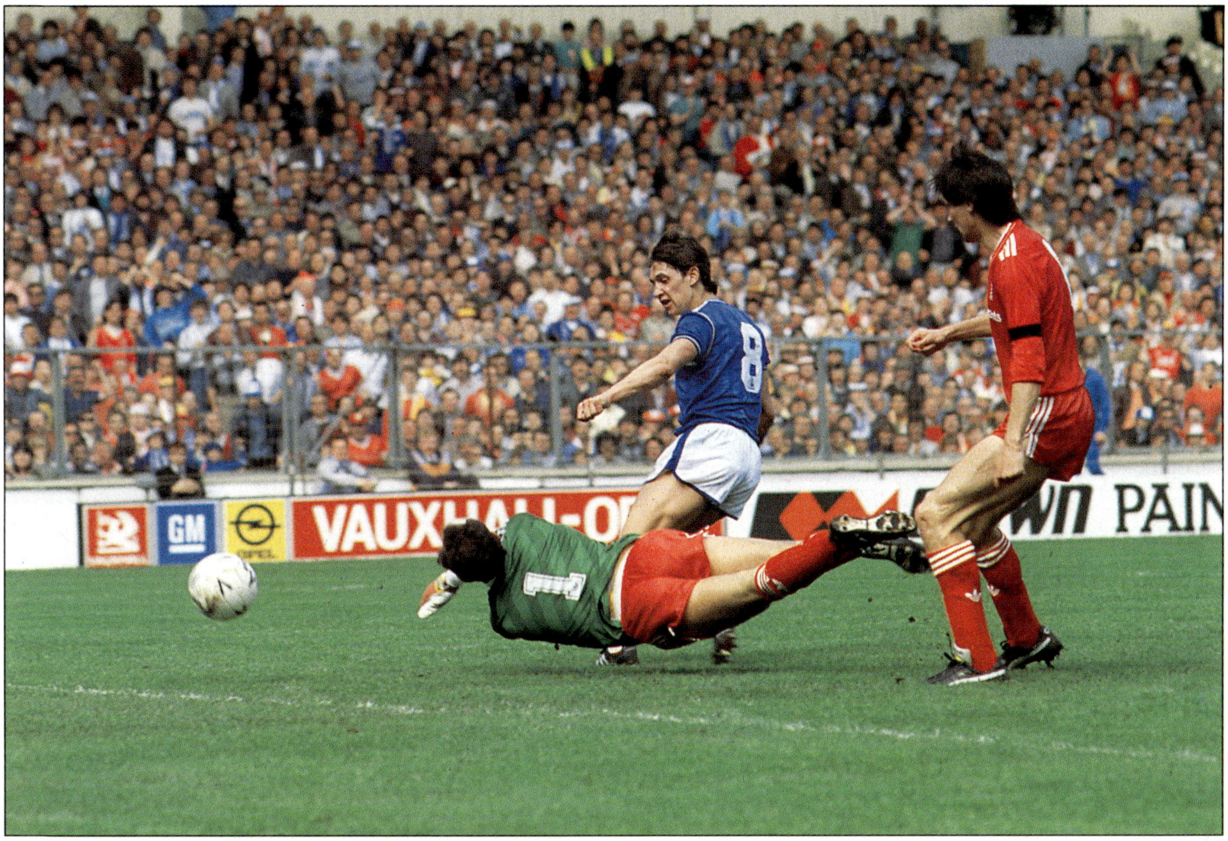
GM
VAUXHALL-OP
PAIN

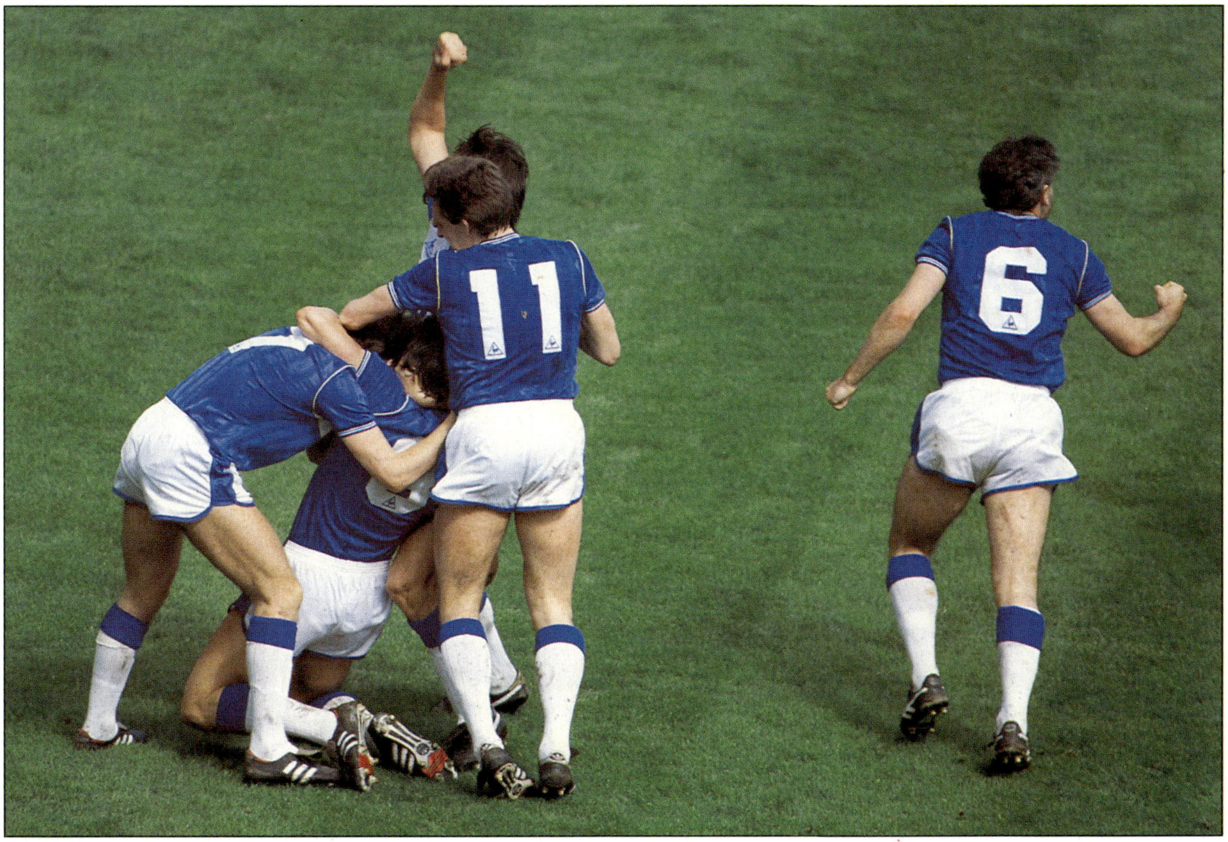

"I thought I had scored the winner, what a sad day,"
comments Lineker on seeing his Wembley goal from another
angle. Neither Grobbelaar nor Hansen could deny him this
goal, but Liverpool responded with three of theirs.

full well where they came from. "I'm only a finisher," he says, smiling at the very word. "I only *like* finishing. But the quality of service is so good at Everton. Gary Stevens, Trevor Steven and Kevin Sheedy all hit such good crosses, my job was to get in front of the defender. Getting there is the important thing."

Getting there, and fitting in. If Kendall admires anything above Lineker's intelligently-timed running it is the unassuming manner of the man. "I knew about his temperament, but even so we were delighted the way Gary came in here," says Kendall.

"He was a record signing for us, but it was not a case of Gary knocking down the door and acting a big star. He came in gently and quietly and got on with the job. He knows where he's going and can be single-minded about that, but he goes about it in a nice way. The players appreciated that. Mind you, if he'd been temperamentally different the players would have knocked that out of him. There's nobody better than the players for doing that."

The Lineker approach, which Kendall suggests is part of his success in Barcelona, is centred on a surprising degree of self-doubt. "I never had incredible belief in myself," he confesses. "When I room with Peter Shilton on England duty I'm amazed at the really powerful self-belief in him. It seems almost an indestructible strength. I know people who succeed in life are supposed to be super confident, but I've never had that."

"I've *wanted* everything that's happened. I'm hungry for every goal, full of ambition. But there's a difference between ambition and belief and much as I dreamed I always told myself, in my innermost feelings, it won't happen. I suppose I appear laid back but I've been fortunate that other people have believed for me at every level."

Out of Leicester's valley of believers, Lineker arrived on Merseyside "expecting to be homesick". He admits: "I wondered how I might cope because Everton are twenty five per cent bigger in every sense than Leicester. But it went well."

Typical Lineker understatement. The Leicester market boy "coped" serenely with his new environment, new team-mates, newly doubled salary, new hotel lifestyle, new rarified crowd atmosphere. Among better players he could no longer be marked as if he was the only danger, yet how could he recreate overnight the chemistry Andy Gray had built up among Evertonians?

He needed, for once, a little time. Lineker thinks he began earning their respect with two goals at Sheffield Wednesday, four days after a hat-trick at Goodison against Birmingham at the end of August. Kendall reflects: "It was longer than that. It took till Christmas for the fans to really accept him, but when the crowd here accept you, you're in."

Arithmetic is a barometer to this acceptance: pre-Christmas Lineker scored six goals at Goodison, after it he struck thirteen. Evertonians, drained by being pipped at the post of a League and Cup double by Liverpool, hoped for solace in a more settled Lineker being quicker off the mark next season.

Gary, and Michelle Cockayne, who had been his girlfriend for six years, had put the finishing touches to a converted barn in Southport they anticipated would be their first home in married life that summer. The furniture moved in, and the Linekers were plucked away to Barcelona. A rueful Kendall reflects on a £2.2 million offer "the club felt they could not refuse" and on a chance "you could not deny any player".

What must Mrs Thatcher have made of it all? Everton, if not the League, might win her nomination for the Queen's Award for Industry. And were the Gary Linekers of this world not so rare, football might bail out Britain's balance of trade deficit. Rarity is the essence of this remarkably quick turnover.

4

ENGLAND'S ANSWER

*Gary Lineker, wearing England strip and holding
his Professional Footballers' Association 1985-86
Player of the Year trophy. The highest accolade
from professionals to a master craftsman.*

Above and left *The full England squad before what Gary describes as "One of my best moments ever, above all other memories." He had just scored his first international goal (against Eire at Wembley) and says: "Once you've scored your first, you know you can get more." Below Training at Bisham Abbey, with Gary Bailey and Chris Waddle.*

Bernabeu Stadium, 18 February 1987: Spain 2, Gary Lineker 4

"I WAS just the man that finished off all the lovely, lovely football we played." Thus did Lineker shrug off scoring all four England goals in a friendly international in Madrid.

Bobby Robson, the England manager, was succinct but less demure: "A joy to see, wasn't it? We have the best finisher in the world."

And Bryan Robson, the nation's captain, put the performance into broader context. "We are close to being a real force," he stated. "We now have the genuine goalscorer that we've always wanted. If there is not much between two teams, someone like Lineker can make all the difference. Mueller did it for West Germany, Platini for France, and if we'd had such a goalscorer in Spain (in 1982) we would have been very, very close to winning the World Cup."

Madrid took Lineker's hot streak to twelve goals in half a dozen internationals, three of which were at the World Cup and two European Championship matches. Never, in the long history of English football, has one man scored so many against such stern opposition. Spain had lost only once in seventeen previous games and rank several classes above Cyprus against whom Newcastle's Malcolm Macdonald hit five goals at Wembley in 1975.

Before Macdonald, the records are sepia-toned. Willie Hall of Tottenham struck five against Ireland at Manchester in 1938, G.O. Smith (Corinthians) similarly went nap against the Irish at Sunderland in 1899, and Steve Bloomer (Derby Co) was credited with five goals against Wales at Cardiff in 1896.

Lineker's four goals were the more remarkable for being scored on hostile ground. The hardest of Spain's hard men knew him well, knew they should watch him like a fox. Three weeks earlier he had sniffed out a hat-trick for Barcelona against Real Madrid, and now the combined might of those club defenders was out to stop him.

Yet the Spaniards played to Lineker's strengths. Miguel Muñoz, their vastly experienced manager, chose two Madrid sweepers and no solid stopper. Perhaps Muñoz thought Gallego and Arteche would read and intercept, but Arteche's renowned Spanish boot could do no harm in the penalty box and Lineker's mobility constantly slipped both men. "Gary's eyes must be rolling at the sight of all those spaces," his Barcelona coach Terry Venables observed early on.

Above *It's that man again, Lineker on the ground at Mark Lawrenson's feet. He got up to score and to collect an Eire shirt as a souvenir of his first goal for England.*

Through the fires of Hampden Park, Glasgow. Lineker is beaten to the ball by Willie Miller in the annual Scotland-England encounter.

Not that Venables could have welcomed the devastating way his centre-forward plundered goals against his own club goalkeeper. Andoni Zubizarreta, a £1 million keeper, had studied Lineker at training each day. He teased that there would be no goal for Gary in Madrid. They fell like this:

No. 1: Bryan Robson, Peter Beardsley and Glenn Hoddle carved the opening and, from Hoddle's chip, Lineker dived between two defenders like a lizard between rocks to head the goal.

Opposite *This way, boss? Gary Lineker demonstrates his heading ability in front of England manager Bobby Robson.*

High rise, USA style. Lineker strains to beat Dan Canter during England's 5-0 victory over the USA in Los Angeles in 1985.

No. 2 and no. 3: Pure Lineker poaching, "easy" six yards finishes from Viv Anderson's inviting header from a rebound when Zubizarreta could not hold Beardsley's shot.

No. 4: A special by Lineker standards. Again his understanding with Beardsley, but this time an audacious finish, allowing Beardsley's pass from the right to cross in front of his own body before volleying, low and left-footed, inside a post. "I just stretched out and knocked it in," insisted Lineker. And he rolled his eyes.

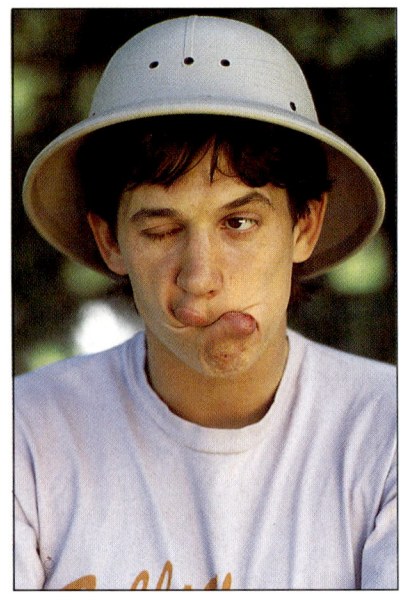

Fun and games in Los Angeles in 1985. Gary proves it is possible to climb above England's towering defender Terry Butcher. His expression (above) is either attributable to the extreme heat or an assessment of England's forthcoming World Cup. Serious work involved carrying the goal, with Alvin Martin, Glenn Hoddle and Steve Hodge at his back.

The style is the man. Opposite *Lineker perfectly balanced, arms artistically spread, eyes fixed on the ball, about to strike at goal.* Right *Putting childhood wicket-keeping practice to the test. Lineker waits behind the stumps, Viv Anderson is the epitome of a Caribbean slip, and together England and West Indian breeding put paid to a Mexico City cricket club eleven by eight wickets.*

In England's dressing-room Lineker, the perfectionist, criticized his night's haul. "He was sick he didn't get six!" explained Bobby Robson. Nice guy Gary: he does for his friend Zubizarreta what buckshot does for a pigeon, and he regrets two that got away. It brings to mind another mild-mannered Midlands sportsman, world 5,000 metres record-holder David Moorcroft, of whom coach John Anderson said:

"Underneath that very pleasant exterior he's an *animal* when he's competing. He gives nothing away."

Lineker considers the comparison, and smiles boyishly. "You mean I see them white sticks and I shoot ruthlessly?" he mocks. "Well you've got to have an inner drive, a hunger for every goal. Selfish? Not necessarily, no. It all happens in flashes of seconds, but I like to think if I see someone in a better position I'd pass the ball." Again that smile, again he reflects. "I'm a finisher. I get most pleasure out of finishing."

The essence of Gary Lineker is that you can see his pleasures from conception to delivery. They happen, as he says, in flashes of seconds, yet

*En route to the World Cup finals. Lineker struck a
hat-trick. First came a warning volley (above),
fractionally wide. Opposite Lineker became air-
propelled to follow up with England's second,
fourth and fifth goals.*

Lineker v John McClelland of N Ireland, Wembley, October 1986.
Left *Gary meets his match as McClelland wins in the air.* Above
*Lineker's revenge was his "best goal for England so far", a left-
foot shot chipped over the goalie, McClelland unable to intercept.*

the impulse is clear and the execution won or lost often before a defender senses the danger. Look closely and you will see him make the same short sprints to the near or far post time and time again, unseen and unrewarded unless the ball is served his way.

He describes goalscoring as a mixture of four essential things: quickness, anticipation, timing, and luck. His first goal in Madrid anticipated a chip so brilliant only Hoddle could have made it. The timing to meet it caught out the defence. And there was in full measure the sheer courage which Lineker did not include in his self-appraisal. If there was luck it was that neither of two defenders, closing from either side like cymbals, clobbered him.

Bravery is not in Lineker's everyday vocabulary, though he knows he has it. He trusts speed and fitness will see him through, he insists football is not as malicious as it may appear, and he touches wood that he will keep popping up as testimony to that fairness.

Besides, he prefers talking about others; one other in particular. In Madrid he switched the point of all interviews to Peter Beardsley's selfless contribution to his goals. "Peter's so full of running, he takes people on, and really gives me the licence of the box," says Lineker.

Praising Beardsley is his party-piece, rather like a comic reminding audiences that the laughs would fall flat without the straight man. It is a heart-felt response on Lineker's behalf, as we saw at Wembley in

October 1986 when the Lineker-Beardsley partnership conjured up his finest international goal.

Lineker's run began from the inside-right position and ended up to the left of Northern Ireland's goal. Beardsley held possession until his partner was about to break towards the penalty area and then gave a pass that demanded every ounce of Lineker's pace, every fibre of guts.

John McClelland, as fast as any British defender, was simply ignored as Lineker brushed past and, in the same seamless movement, struck a left-foot shot from an oblique angle which beat Ireland's goalkeeper after striking the inside of the far post.

"I never thought I'd score a goal like that," breathed Lineker. "At the time I was running away from goal, not thinking about a shot. Out of the corner of my eye I saw that the goalie was not where he should be, so why not try for goal? It surprised me, I don't know about anyone else, because most of my goals come around the six yards box."

But on the field that night, the most demonstrative sign we saw from Lineker was when Beardsley, a player battling to full fitness after early season injury, was taken off seven minutes before the end. Lineker put his hands together and applauded his accomplice every inch of the way to the dug-out – one athlete recognizing another's share of his achievement.

On BBC after the match, Lineker was told his goalscoring was assuming proportions comparable to England's greats. Again he cut across the question: "Provided we (he and Beardsley) both keep doing it there's no reason for our partnership to be changed," he suggested. "Perhaps it was a little unlikely when we were first put together because England traditionally put a big man up with a little man. But Peter's a terrific little player, we decided to give it a go in Russia during a pre-World Cup friendly, and we struck up an understanding right away."

The Lineker-Beardsley duet actually came about in Tbilisi, where England inflicted a most rare 1-0 defeat on Russia at home, because Mark Hateley was unavailable to travel. In his absence, England experimented with a pair who stand 5ft 10in and 5ft 8in (shoulder and chest high to the Colossus of the traditional "British" centre-forward) and discovered our most potent strike force. Not straight away, because Bobby Robson reverted to Hateley and then Kerry Dixon before putting Beardsley (once rejected as a "jockey" by Newcastle) back alongside Lineker in the formation that rescued England's World Cup in Mexico from the third game onwards.

It was from that point that Lineker, coupled with Beardsley, struck the vein of form that invites statistical comparison with the great goal-

Friendly rivalry! Lineker and Mahmoud Salleh get to grips during a 4-0 England win over Egypt in Cairo in January 1986.

Another friend, another far-off place. This time in Tbilisi in March 1986 where, despite Oleg Kuznetsov's over-bearing attitude here, England delivered a very rare 1-0 defeat to Russia on Soviet soil.

Vancouver, May 1986. The World Cup is getting close and, despite appearing to turn his back on Lineker, the Canadian goalkeeper Paul Dolan gets away with this scrambled clearance.

Home for a change, in November 1986. Lineker sneaks past the knee of Farukh Hadzibegic as England beat Yugoslavia 2-0 at Wembley in a European Championship qualifier.

Northern Ireland falling to Lineker at Wembley in October 1986. Top right Lineker opens the scoring in a 3-0 win with a crisp right-foot volley. "Getting there", he says, is the key. Right Goalkeeper Phillip Hughes clutches the ball as Lineker, on almost the same spot, lurks with intent, waiting to pounce on error.

Hold me any way you want to! Turkish defender Abdulkerim shackles Lineker, which probably explains why Gary could only manage three goals for England that day.

Below A goalless World Cup qualifier at Wembley on 13 November 1985. Swedish referee Erik Fredriksson gave a corner kick to England after a Gary Stevens cross was deflected over the bar by Northern Ireland's Alan McDonald. "Until I saw this picture," observes Lineker, "I had no idea that Alan McDonald's hand touched the ball. You can see how close I was, so it's not surprising the referee did not see it either."

Opposite Another close-up of one that got away. The Yugoslav goalkeeper makes a desperate save at Wembley.

scorers. There is, of course, one contemporary prolific talent who, for a year at least, shared the same city as Lineker. Ian Rush as a Liverpool striker stands, or rather runs alone for season by season consistency; Rush went to Juventus in a £3 million deal this summer, and Rush was on Barcelona's shopping list when Lineker was signed.

Yet while Lineker scored twelve times for England in six games, Rush accumulated twelve in twenty nine internationals for Wales. The comparison is totally unfair: a goalscorer, as Rush and Lineker keep insisting, is dependent on the talents around him. Without prompts to serve, as Beardsley does, as Hoddle does par excellence, a striker is barren. Enough said.

The inevitable comparison in English international football is with Jimmy Greaves, who scored forty four goals in fifty seven matches. "Gary has a subtle economy of movement," observes Bobby Robson. "He saves his legs for getting into killer positions at the right time. Denis Law did it to some extent, but Greaves was the best example. Mind you,

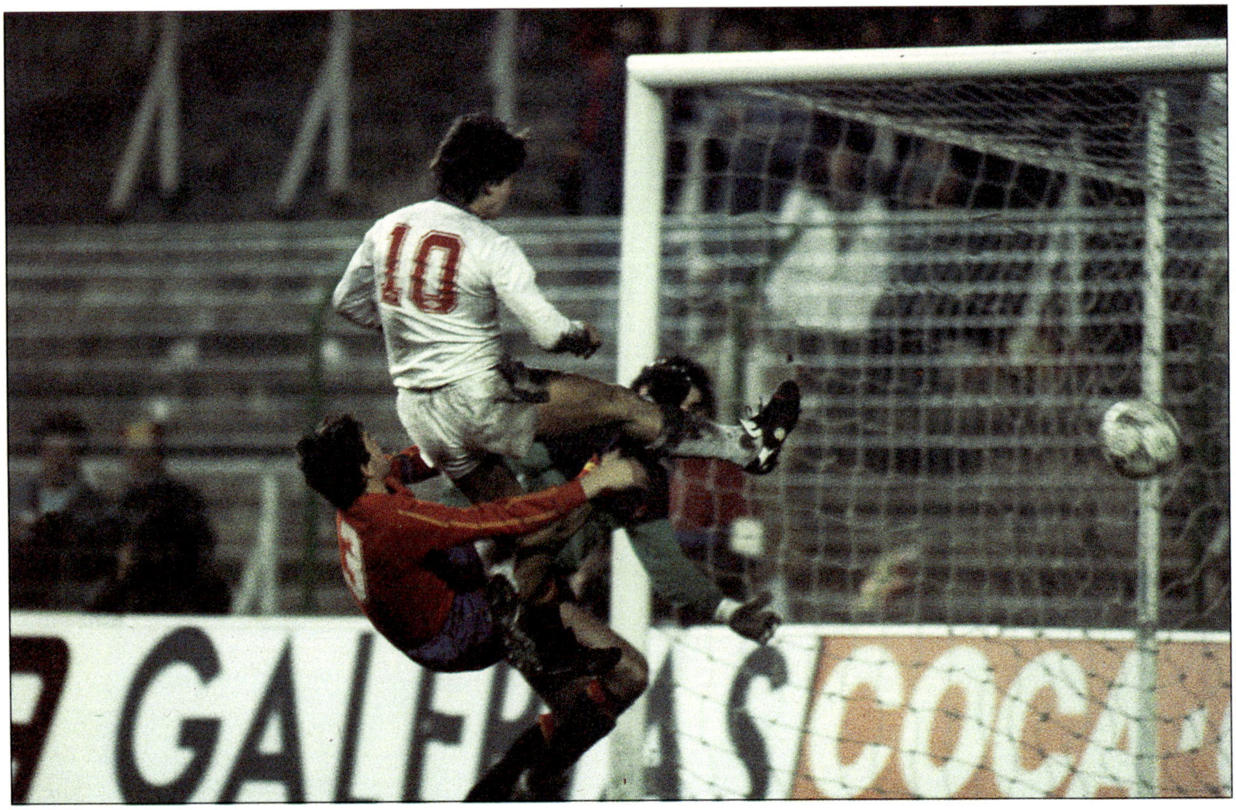

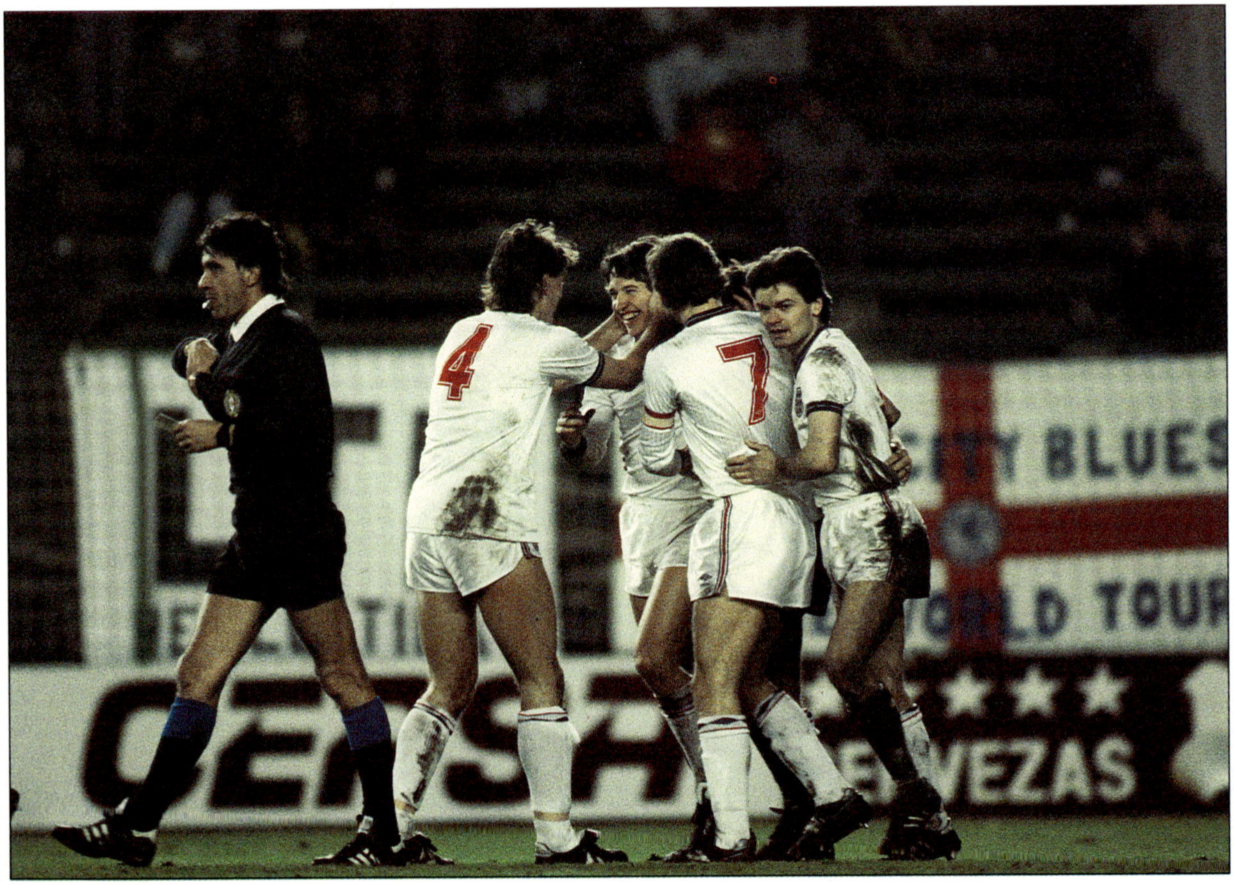

*An away-day celebration, Madrid style. Lineker nips
bravely between Spanish goalkeeper Zubizarreta and
defender Camacho to score the third of his remarkable
four goals in England's 4-2 win in the Bernabeu
Stadium. Glenn Hoddle, Bryan Robson and Steve
Hodge smother him with joy, and Lineker and Robson
have another present for manager Bobby Robson:
a cake for the boss's 54th birthday.*

*You have seen, page 82, the third Lineker goal against Spain, here are the
other three: Top Steve Hodge salutes goal no. 1. Next, Lineker slides in too fast
for defender Chendo. Finally, splitting the Spanish blockade of Arteche and Chendo, Lineker
scores no. 4. Zubizarreta, he says, is still speaking to him!*

if we're asking Gary to emulate Greavesie, he'll need to be in a great team to have the same opportunity."

There are phenomenally high targets to shoot for abroad – Gerd Mueller's 68 goals in 62 internationals for West Germany, Ferenc Puskas's 83 in 84 appearances with Hungary's Magic Magyars, Pele's 95 in 110 Brazilian matches. Those are dreams of a bygone era, one in which Puskas observed: "To be a goalscorer, you must have providers. Every great team has players who can play the piano, and men who will carry it for them."

It is also true, as Bobby Robson tells Lineker, that "The best is yet to come. You are learning all the time, but it will also become harder because you'll be a marked man now."

Marked by history, too. For while the Charltons, Hursts, Hunts, Channons, and Chiverses are well remembered for scoring a goal every second international, Lineker has his sights set higher. Higher, too, than the one in every three appearances on which Haynes and Peters and Keegan and Bryan Robson hit the target.

Lineker need not do the counting, others will keep reminding him. The next marks to tick off are Stan Mortensen's twenty three goals in twenty five games, then Nat Lofthouse's thirty goals in thirty three internationals. But in applying slightly unfair ratios, set in different times, one other factor must be borne in mind. It is that Lineker's international opportunity only truly became fully-fledged during the World Cup in Mexico. In his first eleven appearances from May 1984, he completed the full ninety minutes only four times, either coming on as substitute or being substituted in the rest. He scored six times in what amounts to the apprenticeship of his international career.

These are neither excuses nor regrets. To a boy raised next to his parents' fruit and vegetable stall on Leicester market, the local First Division club and the three lions of England's national shirt were dreams at the end of the rainbow. He went beyond that when he returned to the dressing-room the night of the memorable goal against Northern Ireland. Bobby Robson, the football fan as opposed to the manager responsible for handing out England caps, placed a hand on Lineker's shoulder and enthused:

"What a great goal to score at Wembley. I envy you." Mr Robson, and a few million others.

5

GOLDEN BOOT

*From England, with love. Gary Lineker, the world's
top marksman of 1986.*

YOU may choose to believe that Gary Winston Lineker is nothing special, that he is merely an opportunist lurking in the penalty box to feed off the graft of his colleagues. There is, in that case, no point in you reading this chapter. Its basic premise is that England's World Cup destiny was linked to Lineker's wellbeing.

He came perilously close to not playing a game in Mexico. And (again unless you feel anyone could have done his job) the record suggests that without him England would have caught the first plane home after round one, goalless, winless, disgraced. Football is of course a team game, in which context that suggestion is outrageous. Yet who else was going to score six of England's seven goals? Who else could have claimed the Golden Boot for scoring more than any man, Diego Maradona included?

There has to be a fantasy element in sport, and maybe the role was written for Lineker. Ten days before England's opening match in Monterrey, Gary and Bobby Robson and anyone else who cared about the nation's football spent a couple of hours in despair awaiting the diagnosis on an injured left wrist.

Opposite *A moment of innocence. Lineker and Canada's Randy Samuel, all eyes on the ball, no hint of a foul, collide. Lineker falls on a bone-hard Vancouver pitch, and is taken off to hospital convinced that his left wrist is broken and his World Cup (less than two weeks away) doomed.* Right *The scare is over. The wrist, unbroken, is badly sprained but Gary can play. Meanwhile, skipper Bryan Robson uses his head to keep the plaster dry.*

Before the moment of impact that threatened Lineker's World Cup, he is seen in colour sprinting out of reach of Canada's Terry Moore. After it he lies clutching the wrist, the agony as evident on his face as the concern on physiotherapist Fred Street's. At this moment, both men doubt England's top marksman would be fit for Mexico.

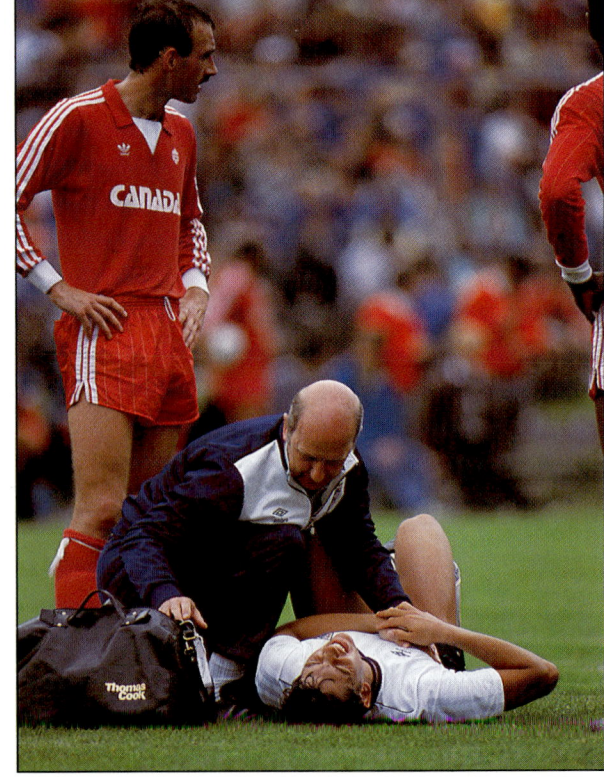

Ambition is a quick healing agent. Once X-rays showed that the wrist was not fractured, Lineker was determined to play and, though he did not score against Portugal (lost 1-0) or Morocco (drew 0-0), you can see from his style on the ball, and the way he screens it from Moroccan Bouyahiaqui, that the plaster cast is the last thing on Lineker's mind.

Opposite *Angles are deceptive. Top Lineker shoots, Portugal goalkeeper Bento is beaten, but the ball is cleared off the line by an unseen defender. Centre Again the odds are on a Lineker goal as he keeps his feet while all around are losing theirs but neither then, nor when Gary stretches out without making contact* (below) *can he end England's barren afternoon.*

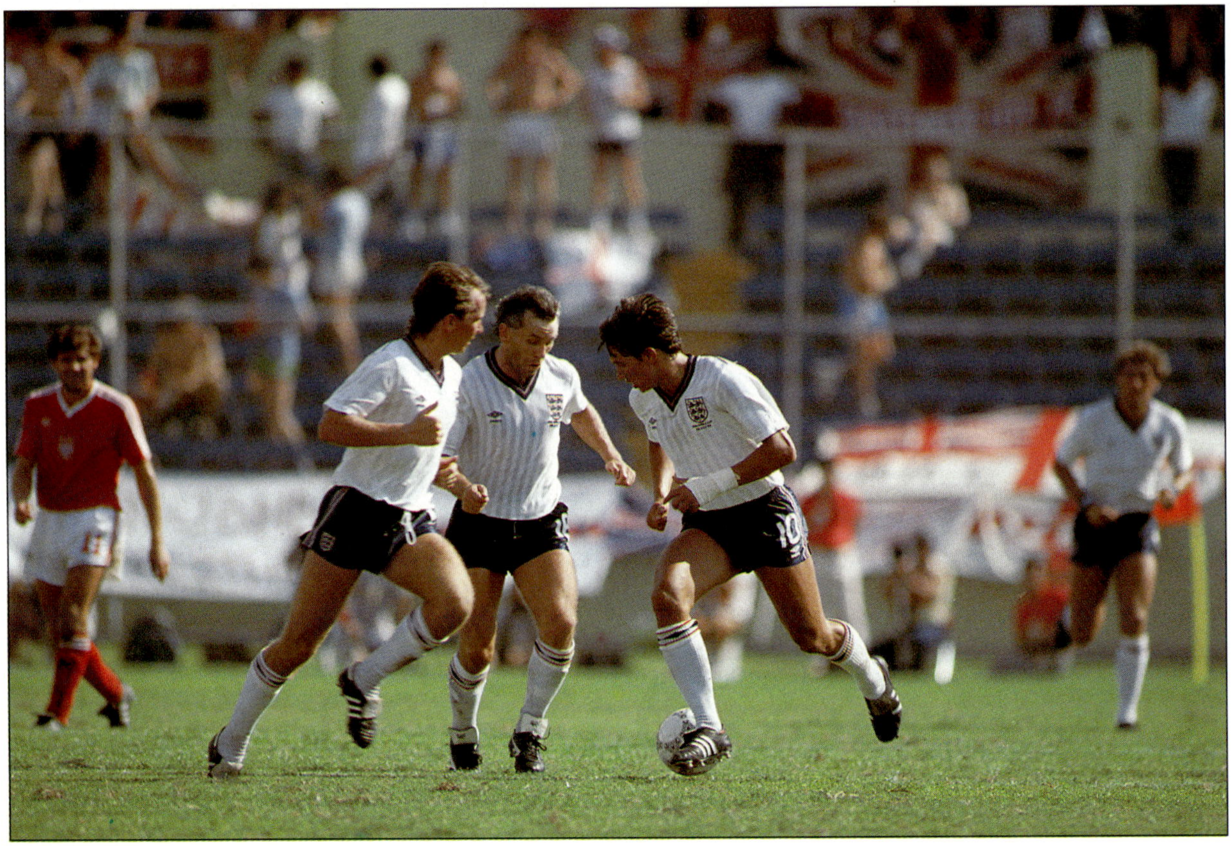

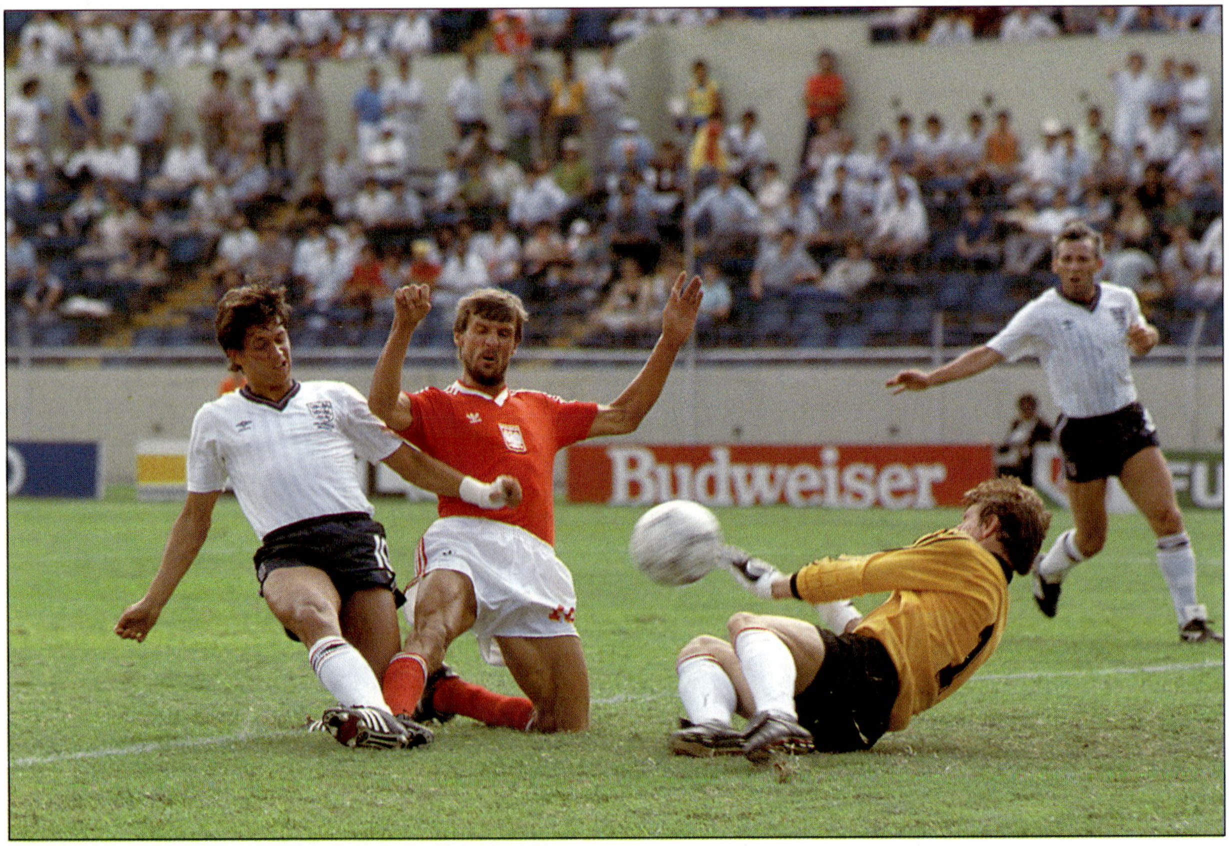
Budweiser

England v Poland: do or die. England's need is now desperate, their collective will perhaps evident (top left) as the Everton trio of Lineker, Reid and Steven converge. At long, long last the goals come: Left Lineker slides in to score under more pressure it would seem than the moments in the previous match where he was denied. Above The second goal left Josef Mlynarczyk helpless and the third sent England into raptures.

The predator's eyes on goal after goal. Defender Stefan Majewski is a fallen, forgotten man (above) as Lineker tries for a fourth goal. This one goes over the bar but, as Bobby Robson withdraws Lineker to keep him fresh for another day under the Mexican sun, he admits: "The night before, Bobby Robson had said: 'Do us a favour son, score four goals tomorrow!' " Gary laughs: "It was a day everything just clicked."

In sequence, that third goal against Poland. Lineker braces himself (left) in anticipation. He swivels and connects sweetly, perfectly with the left boot and there is nothing any Pole can do to prevent the completion of an historic hat-trick.

"Looking back on it," smiles Gary, "the third goal looked on television as though I struck the ball well. In fact, I just scooped it." He, and his country, would do well to reflect on the scoop in Monterrey on the afternoon of 11 June 1986. It saved England's World Cup.

Down to earth in Mexico City, but not in a
harmful way. Lineker (above) finishes on the floor
but his and England's first goal is in the net
against Paraguay.

Lineker had fallen after coming up against Randy Samuel during a warm-up match against Canada in a place off the soccer map called Burnaby. The challenge was innocuous, but the ground was bone hard; indeed, harder than bone it was feared. "I thought I was in trouble," Lineker recalls, "thought the wrist was broken. There was more pain than anything I've had before, and for two hours I was convinced I wouldn't play in the World Cup. But once the hospital told me it wasn't broken that was it, I was determined to play." The joint was badly sprained, he played the entire tournament with it in a light cast, but (with the exception of Maradona) a wrist is not an essential part of a goalscorer's anatomy.

Lineker had expected to enjoy Mexico. Not even a lion hunts under a midday sun as ferocious as Monterrey's, yet while other Englishmen (marathon runners rather than sprinters) broiled to the point of collapse, Lineker relished the heat. "Good for the muscles," he smiled. The smile

*Now, in a more severe sense, the Paraguayans have
their revenge on the goalscorer. Fred Street gesticulates,
the referee is caught up in Latin arguments, and the
perpetrator of a Paraguay chop to Lineker's throat gets
away with things. World Cup cynicism? "I hope the
fellow didn't do it deliberately," says Lineker.*

of a man whose muscles are primed for short, explosive bursts of pace.

For two forgettable matches, the 0-1 defeat to Portugal and the goalless draw against Morocco, nothing came of those bursts. Precious little was created until change was forced on England. Bryan Robson could not go on with a shoulder damaged before he left England, Ray Wilkins was suspended, Mark Hateley and Chris Waddle were "rested". The reformation brought a more direct style from the midfield replacements Peter Reid, Trevor Steven and Steve Hodge, and a more compatible front runner in Peter Beardsley.

"The team played with much better balance, support, width and variation," acknowledged Bobby Robson. Lineker thrived on the promptings of Evertonians Steven and Reid and the effervescence of Beardsley. He scored three times in thirty six minutes – typical, darting, elusive Lineker, preying on gaps in a hesitant Polish defence, unnerving goalkeeper Jozef Mlynarczyk with his cruel timing.

Before his abrupt, painful dismissal, Lineker was the scourge of the Paraguayan penalty box. Opposite He ignores Rogelio Delgado's flailing challenge. Above He finishes off his second and England's third goal of the day.

The other goalscorer? Peter Beardsley, the best partner Lineker has had in an England shirt, and a totally unselfish man who Gary says gives him "the freedom of the box".

Golden moments come and they go. More than any other striker at the World Cup, Gary Lineker knew the joy of scoring (above), the warmth of a team-mate's gratitude (with Steve Hodge, left), and the draining schedule that wears down men in the Mexican sun. Opposite Lineker sleeps en route, between his Everton team-mates Peter Reid (left) and Trevor Steven (right).

The following week, in Mexico City, Lineker and Beardsley ran through Paraguay, Lineker to score twice and Beardsley once. In the Press conference that followed, Lineker surprised old friends and new. Latin journalists, sure they had a story in the apparently vicious way a Paraguayan defender cut Lineker down with a backhander to the throat, were bemused by the tame response: "I hope it wasn't deliberate," said Lineker. Meanwhile, those accustomed to his ways back in Leicester wondered if their man had gone over the top by way of boastfulness: "Yes," he replied to a leading question, "of course it's everybody's dream to finish top goalscorer and I would be lying if I didn't admit I have that ambition."

Gary, Gary, remember your roots boy!

Too late. The ambitious cat was out of the bag. The next match pitted England against Argentina, whose ranks contained a certain little fellow prepared to rise to extraordinary lengths to finish on top. Gary Winston Lineker versus Diego Armando Maradona was a silly attempt to compare the incomparable, though somewhat less fatuous than some journalistic instincts to re-enact the Falklands War through ninety minutes' play.

Bobby Robson, shrewdly alert to the second danger, instructed all his men to avoid being drawn into any conflict. He himself manfully handled the question of the "Hand of God" by which Maradona cheated a goal out of England. And yet, some months later, Robson wandered into the trap

England's one riposte against Argentina. Maradona had scored twice before Lineker set up a rousing finish by outjumping everyone to head this goal. It was not enough, but our man emerged top scorer at the World Cup and received the Golden Boot (left) ahead of Antonio Careca of Brazil and Emilio Butragueno of Spain who took silver and bronze with five goals apiece.

But Diego Maradona, by turns villain, genius and image-maker, was the ultimate winner in the Azteca Stadium. Above *His notorious "Hand of God" goal which denied Peter Shilton, deceived the referee, and effectively put England out of the Cup.* Below *A moment of Maradona theatre as he flies above West Germans Karl-Heinz Förster and Harald Schumacher during the final.* Right *The trophy, the adulation, the acknowledgement of the world's superstar.*

*In the end, we could penetrate Argentina through Lineker
but no one could stop that man! Here was Maradona's
moment of fulfilment, England's last surrender, as the little
Argentine squeezes between Peter Shilton and Terry
Butcher to score his second goal. The anguish on Shilton's
face, the despair in Butcher's lunge, are merely the last
throes of what Gary Lineker, Golden Boot, acknowledges
to be the finest solo goal of the World Cup.*

of measuring Maradona alongside Lineker. "Diego Maradona is a
wonderful, gifted player with great dribbling ability," said the England
manager. "But will he score more goals than Gary?"

Lineker deflected the question with a straight bat. "It's nice of Mr
Robson to say such things," he mused. "But I'm not claiming it." The
truth is, Lineker knows that any comparison between himself and Maradona is "absurd", he has never professed to have "great skills like that".

And, of course, he is right. We remember a Maradona masterpiece
long after we have counted Lineker's statistics. The Argentine is a crea-
ture of melodrama, his goals either artistic or dubious. The Englishman
is a poacher extraordinaire. Lineker scored, and scored well, with his
timely header against Argentina that day in Mexico City. But he will never so long as he lives score such a goal as Maradona's second which left

five sprawling Englishmen in his wake. And he will probably never have the presence of mind, the warped side of Maradona genius, to fist home a goal that his head cannot reach. Indeed, there came such an opportunity late in the game at the Azteca Stadium when a cross fizzed a fraction too high for Lineker, a moment in which using his hand to try to see if the Tunisian referee could be twice deceived never occurred to him. He is a child of the marketplace, not the backstreet.

On paper, Maradona's goals, legal and illegal, beat Lineker's goal before 114,580 spectators. Many of us suspect that, had Lineker indeed reached the second header, Argentina carried enough in reserve to come back again. We shall never know.

Yet there is a quality shared by the Argentine and the Englishman. It is a knack to score goals that grows with the weight of expectation placed on them. Turn up the volume, prime the world's outstanding defenders to try to blot them out, and still they score. You can depend on it.

Why? We accept that a runner, a javelin thrower, a skier gets the best out of himself at a world championship or an Olympics. It is axiomatic that he works up to a peak for that particular day in a two- or four-year cycle. He contends with illness or injury, but that is his challenge.

Yet in a team sport it defies the very logic of planning and sharing that one man should time his effort so much better than the rest. Maradona, we can see, is genius. He cannot be stopped by normal strategy and not always by thugs willing to break his stubby little legs into even smaller bits and pieces.

Lineker remains harder to fathom. The crowd does not frighten him. "I'm never nervous," he says. "The atmosphere at a major snooker tournament (where he accompanies his close friend, the Leicester professional Willie Thorne whenever possible) is miles more intense than anything you get at soccer. It's murder on my nerves just watching." Murder on Thorne, too, to judge by his habit of betraying crowning glory by losing either nerve or concentration and the easy flow of his style.

Lineker has not been known to freeze. Big occasions stimulate him which is why, more than Platini and Elkjaer and Rummenigge and Rossi, he can collect a Golden Boot ahead of Maradona. The Argentine swears it is unimportant, that his captain's hand on the major prize is the name of the game. Maybe. But probe Maradona's mind and you will find, lurking there somewhere, the spectre of Lineker, goalscorer Number One.

6

TERRA FIRMA

Gary Lineker, property of FC Barcelona.

*Showing the colours on foreign soil. Lineker, man
of England, inside the splendid Nou Camp stadium
of Barcelona.*

*Mr and Mrs ... a July match sandwiched between
the World Cup and the move to Barcelona in July
1986. Gary and Michelle Lineker met and married
in their home town Leicester.*

Home for the Linekers is a villa on the grand Parc Belle estate, complete with palms and exclusive swimming pool, a few moments' drive from the stadium.

The man at the piano is a fraud. Michelle is the real player in the Lineker household. Studying the language – or languages because Catalan is different from Spanish – is a task they can share in class or at home.

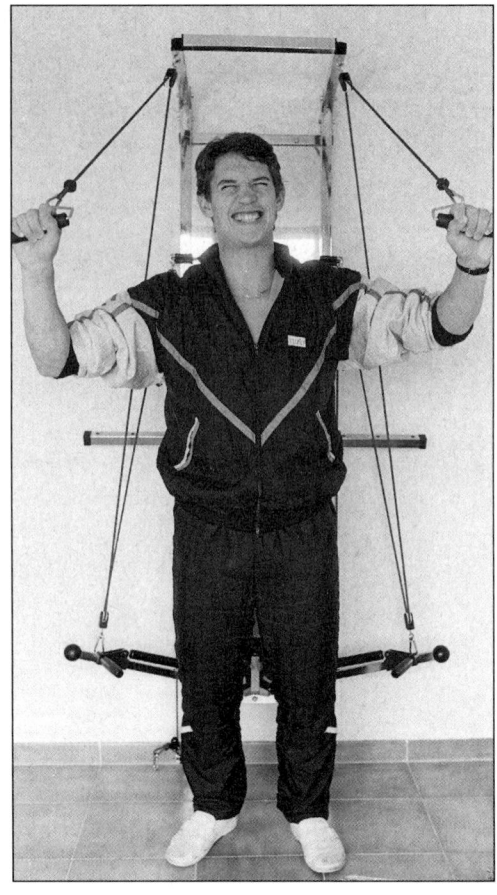

In case Spanish opponents do not stretch Lineker enough, there is all the energetic man could desire on his doorstep – basketball to keep his eye in, a gymnasium below stairs, and lessons from the neighbourhood budding star Marc Bacques.

add the European Cup, dismantled and rebuilt around over £4 million of British strike force, Lineker and Mark Hughes.

The Linekers, equable of temperament, wise and industrious enough to treat the whole episode as a challenge, and so far picking the right straws to bend with and the right ones to ignore, have generally won their first season in Catalonia. They have found friendships away from the game. They have studied the language, acclimatized to the quick, quick slow rhythms of the city, and attacked the entire affair with two maxims: first, that it is they who must adapt, and, equal first, that whatever comes their way will flow principally from achievement on the field.

At the end of the regular championship season, Gary Gol had accumulated seventeen goals from thirty matches, second only to Real Madrid's

Mexican Hugo Sanchez whose penalty tally alone was in double figures.

Hughes, by contrast, dropped out of the team last March and faced a turbulent future. He is more volatile by nature than Lineker, more given to spectacular variations in form, more vulnerable to the shifting moods around Nou Camp. Hughes lost form and confidence at the time Barcelona was engaged in a public show trial brought by Schuster against the club, claiming loss of status and public exposure by his long, languishing relegation to the reserves. The trial put Terry Venables, whose own immediate future was uncertain, in the invidious position of being called as Schuster's witness against the Barcelona club president. A players' manager called to testify against his own paymaster.

The irony was there for all to see at training. Venables was taut and

*Getting to know the environment. The pigeons of
Playa Cataluna, the beach a few miles away, the
marina, and (home from home) the local fruit
market. Both Gary and Michelle come from families
of Leicester market stall holders.*

*No visitor can escape the enormous expectations
of FC Barcelona. Gary manages to look relaxed
amid the opulence of the Nou Camp trophy room.*

withdrawn. Hughes looked bemused and distracted. Lineker got on with
the job and let the politics wash over him. And Schuster? Soccer's interminable enfant terrible, the ultimate rich wastrel, looked what he should
be – a superbly talented athlete, close to his prime, free as a bird in training games, a creator whose range with the ball is stronger and more ex-
quisite even than Glenn Hoddle's. The waste, and the disruptive effect
on one of the two new British imports, was painful to see.

The closest Lineker was drawn into the controversy was to fend off reporters' questions urging him to make comparisons between Hughes and
Steve Archibald, another imported million pound striker who had sat out
half the season surplus to requirements. In Spanish, Lineker calmly,
politely demurred from every question intended to entice from him state-
ments that might hurt either colleague. "Any other questions?" he
asked. "I'm a friend of both Mark and Archie. I prefer what happens on
the field to do the talking."

The ground, too, is resplendent, with seating for 120,000, whose roar represents the ideals of five million Catalans.

Lineker, meanwhile, was using the wisdom of his twenty six years to try to coax Hughes out of his crises of confidence. He was also at home to long-distance calls from Alan Smith, his Leicester successor, who sought advice before his move to Arsenal.

Not that Barcelona was all roses. The club hit a barren spell during which they were overtaken in the table by Real Madrid and put out of Europe by Dundee United. Gary Gol, king of Nou Camp after a tremendous hat-trick over Real, was suddenly harlot after missing a chance in Dundee. "I'm able to take the bad bits quite smoothly," he comments. "I couldn't really take them seriously. To me it's not a miss when I hit the target. In Dundee the ball struck the goalie; the week before I hit one exactly the same and it went through the keeper's legs. I was Gary the hero all week."

In Barcelona, Leicester, Everton or Mexico, people notice only when you score or you miss. "They don't realize all the running you have to do

*All the president's men. Three English, one Welsh, one
Scottish face among the Barcelona pride. Terry Venables and
Alan Harris, manager and coach, stand out in yellow.
Lineker is fourth left on the back row, Mark
Hughes is to his left, and Steve Archibald is
on the extreme left. Hughes and Archibald became
contestants for the second striking role alongside Lineker.*

*Star soccer exports: Lineker and Hughes (Barcelona)
with Mark Hateley and Ray Wilkins who until last
summer earned their keep in Italy with AC Milan.*

*The start of an expensive relationship. Terry
Venables at Nou Camp with his summer signings
of 1986, Lineker and Hughes.*

*Opposite Will you tell them, or shall I? Terry
Venables and Gary Lineker discussing a point in
their mother tongue for a change.*

*Sitting this one out, Gary Lineker and his guest Ray
Wilkins watching the play in a pre-season tournament.*

to try to find spaces. I'm not good at cross-country, I'm a sprinter, always
have been. I can't run all day, and I was pleased when I tried chasing back
during our bad run at Barcelona and Terry (Venables) told me that
wasn't my job, I should stick to my strengths in the box."

Strength is often the word. The Gary Lineker easily knocked off the
ball in apprentice days is now deceptively muscled, especially around the
thighs and shoulders and needs to be in Spain where matches evolve out
of long, tedious, cagey Latin foreplay. The markers stick closer than a
brother. They wrestle, pull shirts, dig ribs, nudge off balance, but (con-
trary to the forewarnings that came via Maradona, Cruyff, Schuster and
Simonsen, great players impaled on Spanish boots in Barcelona) the
kicking is not as physically hard as in England.

It is more an attempt at claustrophobia. A defender tries to envelope

*Training in the mountains of Andorra. "This must have
been early in the session," says Gary. "I'm still smiling!"*

his opponent in a permanent bear hug and for perhaps half an hour
Lineker finds himself foxing and wrestling for a chance to use his pace.
"Because it's so tight, you get a chance to compare yourself one to one for
pace, you gradually find out if you've got the edge but you have to use it
sparingly. In England you look for two or three chances in every game
and they always come. Here you can go two or three games without a
chance, and yet once one goes in it opens up immediately."

Another significant difference is that, whereas in England forwards
hunt in pairs, in Spain he does not look for a partnership. "It isn't possible. You're so far apart all the time that when you get into the box you're
generally on your own."

It is then that he looks for pace to burn, pace which he confides is re-
ceding. "I'm not as quick as I was three years ago," he says. "It's a case of

*Confrontation: Lineker faces up to Real Madrid's
Antonio Camacho (top) and, perhaps unusually, it
is Lineker's turn to chase Camacho (below).*

*The celebrations start. A goal against the
dreaded enemy from Madrid, and a phalanx
of young admirers at the gate.*

Never been booked, but sorely tried in the Latin cauldrons. Above Lineker defends himself against Nimo of Sevilla. Right Ducking the missiles from Real Madrid fanatics dissatisfied by a 1-1 home draw.

too many games, too much stress on the ankles and knees. I can feel it in myself, I'm never as fresh as I'd like to be. I feel a hundred per cent for just the first game of the season, the first ten minutes. After that the little knocks begin to take effect.

"I have a massage at the club, and I always have a bath for two or three minutes before a game. The Spaniards can't believe it, I usually sneak into a little private room, or if there's no bath I get some hot water on my legs just before leaving the hotel. It's a little thing a doctor told me at Leicester because I had trouble with circulation to my feet, they'd sometimes go numb in a game."

Barcelona's Mediterranean climate helps, so do its superb fish restaurants. "I have to watch my diet," he admits, "but because Michelle and I both love the fish here it's a lot better than English food." Life in their four-bedroomed luxury home in grounds with palm trees, a swimming pool and tennis courts is also no hardship, especially after the first five months in a box room of a Barcelona hotel.

Michelle's fashion sense – favouring leather suits styled in Italy and bought in Leicester – pleases the Catalan eye. Gary's perseverance with the language, so that he is at last not found wanting after the second sentence, impresses the radio reporters. And his reading of Orwell's *Homage to Catalonia* is almost complete.

Learning to live, to relax, to laugh the Catalan way is all part of the challenge. All necessary, too. For while there is never a shortage of people suggesting that the six-year contract is just insurance, that no one stays that popular for that long around Nou Camp, it is not lost on Mr and Mrs Lineker that Barcelona is building towards its dream of being the Olympic City in 1992.

The Catalans have waited seven decades to put on this show. Football is the core of their sporting life, and as the Olympics take shape any player who is still around, still doing the business, still knocking in the goals, is going to find himself very popular and very rich. "It's a short life, football," says Lineker, "but I've lots of ambition left. Obviously there's life after football, but as far as I'm concerned my ambitions only go as far as being successful on the field."

The message, from Leicester to Barcelona, from a man nowhere near the end of the sporting road, comes easily: "The big deals all come basically through what I do out there."

A grand night for the Scots, but not the best for Barcelona. Lineker's shot (above) *is crowded out by Dundee United. His stride is dogged by Paul Hegarty* (left), *his jump overpowered by David Narey* (right). *Barcelona lost, both home and away, in the UEFA Cup.*

*Goals, they say, come easily to Gary Lineker.
But look at the running, the effort, the
awareness and the communicating which,
five times out of six, means energy spent just
seeking spaces when the ball never comes.*

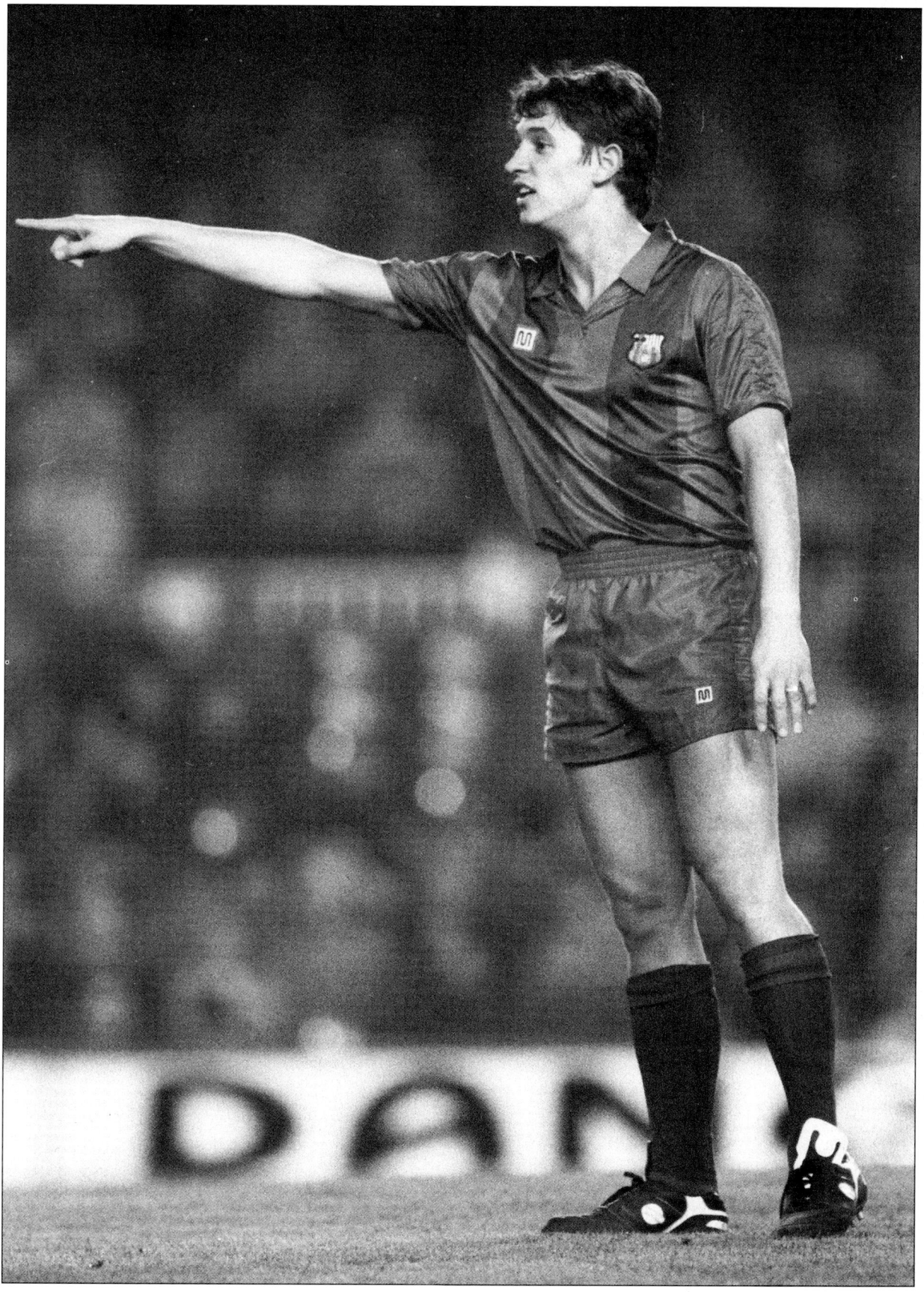

Scoring seventeen goals in his first thirty Spanish league games – second only to Real Madrid's penalty expert Hugo Sanchez – meant sometimes suffocating attention. Above Real Betis employ three defenders to stop Lineker. *Right* His constant marker Alex prepares to use his arms. *Far right* Breathing space is a rare sight.

*Something to smile about? Gary Lineker with the
ultimate in soccer status symbols – new boots designed
with his help, bearing his name, and, provided they
reflect continued success over the coming years, destined
to earn a tidy income supplement. With customary
Lineker timing, he wore the new Quaser boots for the
first time in Madrid the night he scored all four
England goals. Presumably he chose a matching pair,
and not as above the Lineker Gold and the
Lineker Lynx.*

Training, the side of fame Lineker favours least. He stretches the hamstring, he replenishes the inner man, he laughs and jokes … and all with the aim of being fit to burst on match day.

*Predator on the prowl. The ball in
his sights, the body primed for action,
the mind plotting moves far ahead ...
preferably goals.*

*A future to share? Lineker sits in the ruins of the
Montjuic Stadium which will be transformed to
host the 1992 Olympics. Lineker, if he is still part
of the Barcelona scene (which automatically means
his goals not drying up), would be worth millions
to the sports-loving Catalans.*

*Who knows what the future holds? Injury is part and parcel
of the game, the Spanish game particularly. Lineker wisely
is determined to gain what he can from the experience, to
keep the future in mind but play for the present.*

STATISTICS

CLUB RECORD

- Born Leicester 30 November 1960
- Debut 1 January 1979 v Oldham, Filbert Street (W 2-0)
- First goal at Notts County 24 April 1979

Year	Football League apps	goals	FA Cup apps	goals	League Cup apps	goals
Leicester City						
1978/79 (Div 2)	7	1				
1979/80 (Div 2)	16	3	1	0		
1980/81 (Div 1)	9	2	1	1		
1981/82 (Div 2)	37	17	5	2	3	0
1982/83 (Div 2)	39	26 (1 pen)	1	0	2	0
1983/84 (Div 1)	38	22	1	0	1	0
1984/85 (Div 1)	41	24	4	3	3	2

Hat-tricks
11 September 1982 v Carlisle (H), including 1 penalty
23 October 1982 v Derby (A)
14 January 1984 v Notts County (A)
27 October 1984 v Aston Villa (H)
5 January 1985 v Burton Albion (A), FA Cup

Year	Football League apps	goals	FA Cup apps	goals	League Cup apps	goals	Charity Shield apps	goals	Super Cup apps	goals
Everton										
1985/86	41	30	6	5	5	3	1	0	4	2

Hat-tricks
31 August 1985 v Birmingham City (H)
11 February 1986 v Manchester City (H)
3 May 1986 v Southampton (H)

But can he, can any modern striker,
keep it up?

Year	League		Cup		UEFA Cup	
	apps	goals	apps	goals	apps	goals
Barcelona						
1986/87	30	17	1	1	8	0

Hat-tricks (up to 5 April 1987)
31 January 1987 v Real Madrid (H)

ENGLAND RECORD

Date	Venue	Opponents	Result
Leicester City			
26 May 1984	Glasgow	v Scotland (sub)	D 1-1
26 March 1985	Wembley	v Rep of Ireland (taken off)	W 2-1 (Lineker 1)
1 May 1985	Bucharest	v Romania (sub)	D 0-0
25 May 1985	Glasgow	v Scotland (sub)	L 0-1
6 June 1985	Mexico City	v Italy (sub)	L 1-2
12 June 1985	Mexico City	v W Germany (taken off)	W 3-0
16 June 1985	Los Angeles	v USA	W 5-0 (Lineker 2)
Everton			
11 September 1985 (World Cup)	Wembley	v Romania (taken off)	D 1-1
16 October 1985 (World Cup)	Wembley	v Turkey	W 5-0 (Lineker 3)
13 November 1985 (World Cup)	Wembley	v N Ireland	D 0-0
29 January 1986	Cairo	v Egypt (taken off)	W 4-0
26 March 1986	Tbilisi	v USSR	W 1-0
24 May 1986	Burnaby	v Canada (taken off)	W 1-0
3 June 1986 (World Cup)	Monterrey	v Portugal	L 0-1
6 June 1986 (World Cup)	Monterrey	v Morocco	D 0-0
11 June 1986 (World Cup)	Monterrey	v Poland (taken off)	W 3-0 (Lineker 3)
18 June 1986 (World Cup)	Mexico City	v Paraguay	W 3-0 (Lineker 2)
22 June 1986 (World Cup)	Mexico City	v Argentina	L 1-2 (Lineker 1)
Barcelona			
15 October 1986 (Euro Championship)	Wembley	v N Ireland	W 3-0 (Lineker 2)
12 November 1986 (Euro Championship)	Wembley	v Yugoslavia	W 2-0
18 February 1987	Madrid	v Spain	W 4-2 (Lineker 4)
1 April 1987 (Euro Championship)	Belfast	v N Ireland	W 2-0
29 April 1987 (Euro Championship)	Izmir	v Turkey	D 0-0
19 May 1987	Wembley	v Brazil (taken off)	D 1-1 (Lineker 1)

Number of goals: 19
Number of games: 24 (four as substitute)